# TERRACE
## HOUSES
### IN AUSTRALIA

TREVOR HOWELLS    COLLEEN MORRIS

# TERRACE
## HOUSES
### IN AUSTRALIA

LANSDOWNE

Published by Lansdowne Publishing Pty Ltd
Level 1, 18 Argyle Street
The Rocks NSW 2000, Australia

First published 1999

Authors: Trevor Howells and Colleen Morris
Principal Photographer: Georgie Cole

Publisher: Deborah Nixon
Production Manager: Sally Stokes
Editorial Coordinator: Joanne Holliman
Designer: Gayna Murphy, Greendot Design
Copy Editor: Derek Barton
Illustrator: Jann McKay

Set in Times New Roman PS 11.5/17pt on QuarkXPress
Printed in Singapore by Kyodo Printing Pte Ltd.

National Library of Australia Cataloguing-in-Publication Data:

Howells, Trevor, 1949– .
    Terrace houses in Australia.

    Bibliography.
    Includes Index.
    ISBN 1 86302 649 5.

    1. Architecture, Domestic – Australia – History.  2.
    Architecture, Domestic – Australia – Conservation and
    restoration.  I. Morris, Colleen.  II. Title.

728.3120994

TO THE MEMORY OF MY LOVING MOTHER
9.XII.1919 – 13.XI.1998
TJH

ET IN ARCADIA EGO

ENDPAPERS: Tessellated, encaustic ceramic tiles were used widely for
garden paths, verandahs and hall floors of terrace houses throughout
the second half of the nineteenth century.

PAGE 1: The decorated parapet became a hallmark feature of the
Victorian terrace house. In this Federation terrace a rich mixture of
unpainted face brickwork has been crowned by a highly ornamented
pediment over the windows.

PAGE 2: During the nineteenth century, factory-made cast-iron
balustrade panels became popular as changes in technology made
them more affordable. The rich decorative patterns were enhanced by
simple, bold colours such as this Indian red.

THIS PAGE: The terrace house was ideally suited for both level and
hilly sites. In Davenport Street, Hobart, this modern, though
appropriate, garden frames one of a row of terraces which step down
the slope with ease.

# Contents

# The Evolution of

## TERRACE HOUSES

For the majority of Australians the terrace house is most closely associated with the nineteenth century, and indeed terrace houses did enjoy their greatest popularity as a residential building form during the second half of the nineteenth century. These were the days before the arrival of the motor car and public transport systems so it was necessary for most people to live close to their place of work. The terrace house, with its efficient use of land, provided the best solution to this requirement.

Terrace houses are found throughout Australia in the cities and larger towns, especially Melbourne and Sydney, and to a lesser extent Perth, Hobart and Launceston. The Australian terrace house developed from its eighteenth-century English predecessors which consisted of rows of attached houses of between two and five storeys, depending upon the wealth of the owners. One major Australian variation was the shaded verandah, which was rarely a feature of the English terrace house although they sometimes had small projecting balconies at first-floor level.

## CLASSIFYING TERRACE HOUSES

Applying architectural styles to terrace houses has always been problematic for Australian architectural historians. Richard Apperly, Robert Irving and Peter Reynolds in their book *A Pictorial Guide to Identifying Australian Architecture* observed that '… there is no agreed terminology for architectural styles in Australia'.

**ABOVE:** Photographed in 1871 soon after its completion, Pembroke Terrace comprises the first six houses in this row and, along with the neighbouring houses, is a typical example of a stark early terrace house streetscape close to the city centre. Pembroke Terrace still survives on the corner of Cleveland and Buckingham streets in Sydney's Surry Hills.

**RIGHT:** With the great wealth generated by the Gold Rushes, swagger and ostentation found their perfect vehicle for architectural expression in the overblown Boom style. This splendid example in Melbourne's Fitzroy attempts to pass itself off as small Italian palazzo and shows no restraint in proclaiming its owner's wealth and social status—or aspirations.

The nineteenth-century terrace house contributed to the character of Sydney's early community. This c.1879 photograph of Cumberland Street in The Rocks, Sydney, looking southeast, shows a great harmony of diverse scale, materials and building types, including terrace houses of one and two storeys, freestanding cottages, saw-toothed bond stores and warehouses. Banana trees, as seen in right foreground, were planted in colonial times because they were both productive and ornamental.

Authors, therefore, have to adopt a rather loose and encompassing approach to classifying the different styles. The timescales used in this book for different periods recognise the tendency for the continuation of a style after the high-water mark of its popularity has been passed. As well, these chronological markers have been used to group together houses of similar stylistic characteristics, common and typical of their time.

The five broad architectural styles used—Georgian, Regency, Early Victorian, Boom style, and Federation—cover the period from the building of the earliest terrace houses in Australia until their demise around 1920. No matter how pedantic and precise the architectural historian might be in drawing the boundary between one style and the next, the buildings themselves, their occupants, designers and builders are too idiosyncratic to fit perfectly into simple descriptive categories. Exceptions always seem to abound and the perceptive reader is invited to discover his and her own.

## EARLY AUSTRALIAN TERRACES

The great majority of early terrace houses dating from the Georgian period (1820–1850) were either single- or double-storeyed, and almost without exception lacked verandahs or balconies. The simplicity of these humble examples, which are found only in New South Wales and Tasmania, is testament to the difficulties experienced in establishing colonial settlements which permitted no unnecessary architectural ornamentation.

By the time the Regency terrace (1830–1860) appeared, greater wealth and aspirations to acquire fashionable tastes and style provided the impetus for the development of terrace houses suitable for both rich and poor. Major contributions during this period were the introduction of the verandah and the balcony.

The first gardens in the colonies were necessarily utilitarian but as the earliest communities (those around the settlements of Sydney and Hobart) became more established, gardens based on English prototypes

RIGHT: The origins of the Australian terrace house were necessarily modest. Many small single-storeyed terraces contained no more than three or four rooms. Most surviving examples of early Georgian terraces are found in Tasmania's larger towns and cities. They were often built on hilly or cheap sites, as can be seen in South Hobart, and their repetitive geometry readily accommodated falling terrain with elegant ease.

CENTRE RIGHT: In the early days there was often no clear distinction between the attached cottage and the terrace house. This freestanding Georgian cottage in South Hobart has a hipped roof over a symmetrically balanced central corridor with rooms on either side. It was built next to another, and this became the forerunner of planned terrace houses. The olive tree, lavender and geraniums in the garden are sympathetic to the period of the house.

BELOW: A ground-floor shop with a residence above was common in Victorian times. This corner location in Kent Street, Sydney, would have been highly sought as its customers would include sailors from ships moored at nearby Walsh and Cockle bays and local residents.

BELOW RIGHT: Like its Georgian antecedent, the early Victorian terrace displayed little exterior decoration. These four houses in Sydney's Atherden Street, The Rocks, make up one of the shortest terraces in Australia.

became increasingly sophisticated. Stylistically, the more ornamental gardens show remarkably little variation throughout the Regency, Victorian and Boom styles of the nineteenth and early-twentieth centuries, with only subtle differences in size and the introduction of new materials, plants and decorative elements.

By the 1830s simple layouts for the front gardens of terrace houses were often published in the books and magazines of the influential Scottish gardening writer John Claudius Loudon, and these served as pattern books for Loudon's British and Australian audiences. Loudon recommended the circle as the simplest and most effective shape for garden beds and a centrally placed circular garden bed became a common choice for the confined space of the front gardens of nineteenth-century terrace houses. The adventurous chose variations of Loudon's more sophisticated suggestions, which included locations for urns or fountains. Garden beds were often edged with a low hedge such as box.

## LATE NINETEENTH CENTURY

The Victorian age was a period of great economic development and saw a rapid increase in the urban population. The early Victorian terrace house (1850–1870) was quickly adopted in most Australian cities as the typical form of housing. In this period the kitchen or service wing developed as an almost constant element of terrace house planning, along with the use of decorative cast iron applied to verandahs and balconies.

In the wake of the great wealth generated by the 1850s gold rushes, the prevailing mood of optimism in the 1870s and 1880s encouraged a richer, more florid and highly decorated language of architecture. The architectural fruits of the era, appropriately named the 'Boom style', are most apparent in the increase in size and scale of the houses and the lavishness of embellishment added to them. Although the Boom style terrace was built throughout Australia, it was in Melbourne that the most extravagant and magnificent examples were erected.

During the second half of the nineteenth and into the twentieth century the use of decorative brick edge or terracotta garden edging tiles became more fashionable.

Back gardens remained essentially utilitarian with space used for hanging washing, the outdoor lavatory and the occasional fruit tree, usually a lemon. Geraniums grew in pots or, more often, in containers recycled to the garden after their usefulness as teapot, bucket or kerosene tin had ended. If there was room, a chicken coop or a vegetable patch completed the picture. Greater horticultural sophistication was introduced to some back gardens in the latter half of the nineteenth century with the addition of rock gardens, greenhouses, or ferns, commonly the native staghorn and elkhorn which could be elevated on a wall or tree stump.

## FROM RECESSION TO RESTORATION

The financial crash of the early 1890s had a sobering influence on Australian society and its aftermath was a less ostentatious and more modest legacy in architecture. The Federation terrace (1890–1920) reverted to the scale and character of the typical double-storeyed early Victorian terrace, albeit in a new set of clothes which swapped terracotta for slate, face

Victorian terrace houses, such as this row in The Rocks, Sydney, adopted many ingenious devices for maximising the use of available space. Perhaps the most successful was the cantilevered or 'sweated' balconies built over the street footpath. These provided shelter to the passing public as well as increased floor area to a very small terrace plot. The dormer windows allowed otherwise wasted roof spaces to be used for additional bedrooms.

**ABOVE:** The scale of Melbourne's Boom-style terraces was without equal in Australia. Rochester Terrace in South Melbourne's St Vincent Place demonstrates how a commodious terrace with grand, colonnaded façades, can produce urban environments of high quality, particularly with an extensive, part-private, part-public garden.

**RIGHT:** The transition from one style to its successor caught many builders unprepared. Launceston's Cameron Street terraces are a mixture of early Federation and Boom style. The rich, red brickwork of Federation replaced stucco, but the cast iron and other details, such as the stuccoed window mouldings, are essentially Boom-style flourishes.

**BELOW:** As the Federation style was fully embraced, decorative cast iron was replaced by turned, fretted or even carved timber verandah posts and balustrades. This detail from a short row of terraces in Beaufort Street, West Perth, shows the fruits of the woodworker's lathe at their robust best.

In the 1950s when the majority of Australians saw nineteenth-century houses as slums worthy only of demolition, non-Anglo-Saxon immigrants savoured their inherent urbanity. Many, especially Greeks and Italians, bought them as reminders of the housing they had 'back home', and because they were cheap. Swiss-born painter Sali Herman often painted terraces; his work, such as *The French Flag* (1963), played an important role in helping others to value Australia's terrace houses.

brickwork for highly modelled stucco, and painted timberwork for decorative cast iron. The accumulated social ills of Australia's cities saw many areas of terrace housing descend into decay, squalor and disease. By the 1920s the terrace house was widely regarded as a building type which inevitably degenerated into slums, and as a consequence was outlawed under new building regulations or was superseded by the appearance of the freestanding suburban bungalow.

However, from the 1960s onwards increasing numbers of disenchanted outer-suburban residents began the flight back to the inner city, rediscovering both the convenience of living close to the centre of town and the charm of the nineteenth-century terrace house. The boom in house renovation and restoration, which began then, continues unabated to the present. Throughout Australian cities at that time planning authorities and

local councils began to take notice as planning and building regulations were relaxed to permit the re-emergence of the contemporary terrace house—a process that has continued into the 1980s and 1990s. Often built in older inner-city areas designated as protected historic precincts, many of Australia's best architects have created terrace houses for our own times.

Few changes took place in the back garden during the early part of the twentieth century. Since then, however, changes in sanitary facilities have changed the way garden space is used. As the use of 'coppers' for washing clothes declined and were replaced so did the need to store wood. The lavatory was also moved inside the house. Fruit trees died and were not replaced. More recently still, the back garden has continued to evolve as residents place emphasis on the need for outdoor living and dining areas, and more ornamental surroundings.

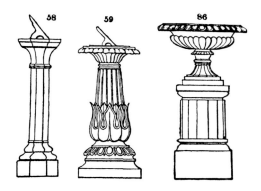

**ABOVE:** These two sundials and the artificial stone urn, or 'tazza' as this shape urn was called, featured in John Claudis Loudon's publications. This popular tazza-design urn was recommended for creeping plants and was produced in artificial stone and cast iron by a number of companies throughout the nineteenth century.

**RIGHT:** A group of children and their dog pose in front of ferns mounted on a shed wall. Elkhorns and staghorns, epiphytic ferns from the genus *Platycerium*, were popular in the confined gardens of terraces. They grew easily, and could be either tied to trees or mounted on board and attached to walls. A tree fern grows below the staghorns and elkhorns.

**ABOVE:** These illustrations are of plans drawn up to provide ideas for front garden layouts. The small circles represent positions for urns, statuary or centrally placed fountains. The garden beds and borders could be edged with stone or brick kerbs and the walks paved or laid with gravel.

**RIGHT:** Federation did little to change the fundamental characteristics of Victorian design. A preference for unpainted red brick over stucco and elaborate timberwork instead of cast iron was the major difference. Apart from the fact that the stucco has been replaced with face brickwork, this 1890s terrace in Sydney appears to be a rather undistinguished and largely undecorated Boom-style house.

Built in 1846, Fitzroy Terrace in Redfern represents the largest and grandest surviving row of Georgian terrace houses in Sydney. Here one can readily see how symmetrical composition took precedence over other considerations. The emphasis of the central house was achieved by pulling the façade forward and raising the roof line in the manner of a simplified classical temple form without columns. The gardens of these terraces are relatively recent additions. They provide a peaceful setting in a busy neighbourhood.

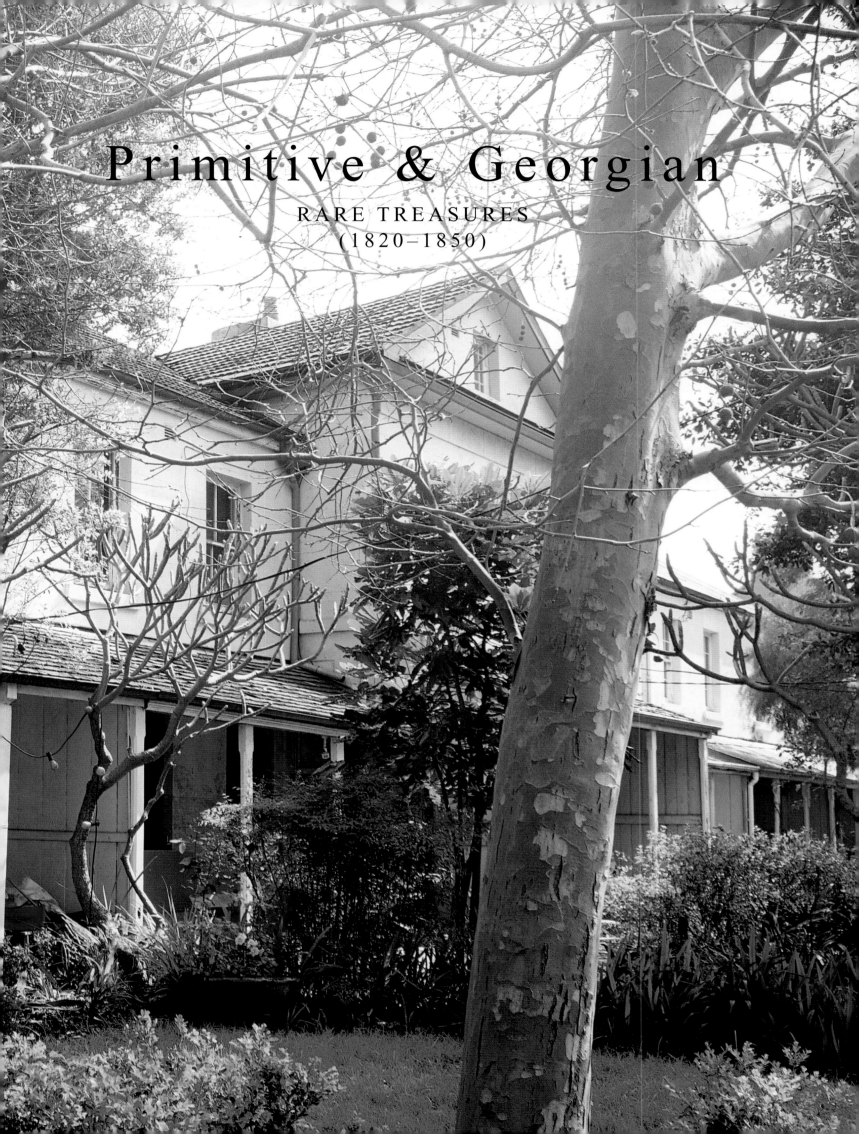

# Primitive & Georgian

## RARE TREASURES
### (1820–1850)

Defining what constitutes the earliest terrace houses in Australia presents certain problems. If the Australian terrace house is, as David Saunders has observed, '...a story...not about architects...' the history of the earliest examples is largely an account of anonymous builders and residents. Drawing the line between a row of attached cottages and a distinctive terrace house type is also not clear cut. The English cottage was often attached as well as freestanding, whereas the English terrace house always shared common party walls. In colonial Australia the cottage was nearly always a single-storey house of modest proportions, freestanding from its neighbours with gardens at the front and back.

Robert Moore and Sheridan Burke in *Australian Cottages* have identified relatively rare examples of the attached cottage in Battery Point, Hobart, and in Burra Burra, South Australia. The earliest or most primitive terrace houses in Australia might just as readily be described as 'attached cottages'. A rare surviving example, 'The Ark' (later called 'Glover Cottages') falls into this category. Built in 1823 of unplastered Sydney sandstone rubble, the masonry represents the oldest surviving example of the attached cottage, and this became the precursor of the terrace house. Like almost all terraces of this era, they were built right up to the street alignment leaving no space for a front garden. The use of the hipped roof in preference to the gable and the appearance of the central hallway suggested a freestanding house rather than the row-house type.

## ARCHITECTURAL CHARACTERISTICS

Because defining the Georgian terrace in Australia has its difficulties, rather than attempt to confine the Georgian terrace house within a specific time span this book will consider the Georgian terrace house as one which displays consistent and particular stylistic and architectural characteristics as well as falling within a general time span. Architectural styles, especially when applied to more modest examples of a building type, have tended to linger after their general period of popularity.

Whether this is due to a preference for established styles in the isolation of rural backwaters or to old-fashioned builders set in their ways, the sharp-eyed architectural detective will discover numerous terrace houses built after the era of a style's fashionable currency.

Of all the manifestations of the terrace house in Australia, the Georgian most closely resembles its English counterpart. These houses can be readily identified by their characteristic use of certain materials, a relative lack of applied architectural detail of mouldings, and a direct but fundamental concern for well-balanced proportions and symmetries.

The general hallmarks of the Georgian terrace embrace a modesty of scale, discreet use of materials, a chaste application of decoration and a simplicity of form. Flashy ornamentation and the use of elaborate architectural elements such as finials, parapets and geometric complexity had to wait until later generations of builders and householders.

## EXTERNAL FEATURES AND ROOF LINES

Although the range of materials used by the typical Georgian terrace-house builder was quite limited, a substantial degree of subtle variation could be achieved through the skilful use of proportion and fine joinery. The external walls were most often of brick, sometimes of stone masonry—whether of the more expensive and sophisticated regular coursed ashlar or cheaper, cruder irregular rubble work.

The most complicated and sophisticated elements of the building construction were the visible timber joinery of doors, windows and shutters which, if removed, left little more than well-proportioned brick boxes with a regular series of openings. Delicate mouldings were applied to small but critical elements, such as the glazing bars of windows and the recessed panels of doors. Protection from the weather for external joinery was achieved by the use of oil paints: off-white and cream colours for the windows, bronze, greens or another deep colour for the doors and shutters.

ABOVE: Even the shallowest of front gardens could soften the bare-faced austerity which characterised the average row of Georgian terraces built hard up against the public footpath. In De Witt Street, Hobart, for instance, where the value of land was not as high as in Sydney, developers' speculative housing ventures often allowed modest gardens.

RIGHT: The primitive Georgian terrace was often very small, as this row of single-storeyed, two-roomed terraces in Sydney's Burton Street, Darlinghurst, attests. Built around 1845, dwellings of this scale were intended for workers of modest means. To increase interior space, owners today have combined two houses into a single residence.

**LEFT:** The New South Wales Historic Houses Trust maintains Susannah Place at 60–64 Gloucester Street, The Rocks, as a museum. Miraculously, it has been preserved to mirror exactly the domestic life of the working poor. Eating as well as cooking were the primary functions of the kitchen as the accommodation of the house could not afford the luxury of a dining room. The original kitchen with its cast-iron stove has survived to a remarkable degree, although the wooden sink and piped water are later additions.

**BELOW:** The lean-to roofed rooms usually located at the back of the Georgian terrace contained the domestic service functions—kitchens, then later bathrooms. At Susannah Place the kitchens were built in the timber-clad rooms at the rear with the laundry below, next to the outside water closet.

**BOTTOM:** Built in 1844, Susannah Place terrace in The Rocks, Sydney, is unusual in that it has a carved sandstone plaque recording its name and date of construction. Most rows of Georgian terrace houses remain anonymous and unnamed.

**ABOVE:** The typical ground floor front room of a Georgian terrace, as can be seen at 60 Susannah Place, was commonly called the parlour. Here the remarkably intact details have been furnished in the manner of the 1840s. As it was usual for the occupants to receive and entertain only in the parlour, the greatest effort and money, as much as the purse would allow, was spent in furnishing and decoration.

The principal bedroom at 60 Susannah Place was a suitably modest affair. Clothes were kept in curtained wall niches, saving money and spaces; summer flies and mosquitoes were kept at bay from the matrimonial bed by muslin hangings strung on four posts.

Roof lines usually consisted of a simple continuous gable running parallel to the street. Though none survive intact, the roofs of Georgian terraces and other houses were invariably covered with split timber shingles, usually from native river she-oak or casuarina species, which weathered to silver-grey in the harsh Australian sun. It was these shimmering shingle roofs, perhaps more than any other element of the Georgian house, which fired the eye of architect and writer William Hardy Wilson. His lyrically seductive renderings of the roofs of Georgian and Regency houses to illustrate his book *Old Colonial Architecture in New South Wales and Tasmania* successfully captured their gentle and dappled patterns of light and shade. Sadly, the limited life expectancy of a shingle roof never matched the durability of masonry and joinery, and the ever-present danger of fire led to its progressive disappearance from the middle of the nineteenth century. Depending upon

time, place and budget, they were gradually replaced by corrugated iron sheeting, slate, or Marseilles pattern terracotta tiles. Old roofs can often be found beneath later Victorian recladding, when corrugated iron sheeting was applied directly over the original shingles for reasons of expediency as well as the added bonus of built-in thermal insulation.

The general texture of the materials used on the exterior of the Georgian terrace consisted of an interplay between the roughness of the weathered shingles, the gentle texture of the hand-pressed sandstock brickwork and the clarity of the smoothly finished joinery, all delineated sharply in the light.

### INTERNAL FEATURES

Inside a Georgian terrace the finishes were less three-dimensional in appearance than the external finishes, and responded to softer patterns of light. Here the

A grocery shop was often incorporated into a row of terraces. At 64 Susannah Place the general grocer's store opened its doors for business in 1845 and traded without interruption until 1930. Like the corner pub, the doorway was invariably placed at the corner, cut on a splay, to attract custom from all directions.

**ABOVE:** In Tasmania, early terrace houses were little more than Georgian cottages sharing a common roof. Although now referred to as terraces, these two houses in De Witt Street, Hobart, are essentially cottages. A passage to the back garden separates the houses. The roses in this garden add a period touch as roses were highly sought for early terrace house gardens.

**LEFT:** Without a sloping site, these early Georgian terraces in Davey Street, Hobart, rely on the door and window openings to enliven the façade.

**BELOW:** Built to be functional and inexpensive, the primitive terrace could lay little claim to great architectural distinction. The bare essentials of Mill Cottages in Davey Street, South Hobart, reflect their era.

**BELOW:** Although the majority of Sydney's early terraces were built of brick, sandstone was frequently used. This row of houses in Paddington's Underwood Street was amongst the area's first, built in the early 1840s by and for the masons responsible for the nearby Victoria Barracks. Now covered with corrugated steel sheeting, the original roof was clad with split casuarina or she-oak timber shingles.

Tasmania's Georgian style at its most modest is seen in this terrace in Forest Road, South Hobart. Despite the Georgian preference for axial symmetry, the arrangement of the window and front door reflects practical needs rather than classical geometry. The house is barely three metres wide and the corridor runs adjacent to the party wall. This is one of the fundamental features of terrace house planning which persisted throughout the nineteenth century. The planting of productive fruit trees in the garden was common in colonial times. Almond, peach, pear, fig, loquat and quince featured in the nursery catalogue published by Daniel Brunce in the *Hobart Town Courier* in 1836.

palette of materials changed a little to allow smooth-textured wall and ceiling finishes. Exposed brickwork gave way to smooth-line plastering on the walls and ceilings. Depending upon wealth and aspirations to fashion, the householder either painted or papered the walls—wallpaper was generally a luxury in the Georgian period. Cornices and ceiling roses of lime plaster run in-situ were sometimes added to the more important rooms where guests were received.

If elegance and well-developed proportions were evident in the arrangement of the doors and windows and in the joinery details, the planning of rooms in the typical Georgian terrace house was rather more straightforward. Depending upon scale, the front door led either into a short hall or directly into the parlour. Immediately behind the parlour, usually the only room in the house where it was intended guests and visitors would be received, stood the dining room. Both rooms normally contained fireplaces, located back-to-back or

arranged along the party wall opposite the front door. In line with the dining room the hall usually dog-legged to accommodate the stair to the first floor. Beyond the stair lay the kitchen and scullery (if there was no cellar) and small backyard with storage for wood or coal. Where a slope of the ground allowed, the kitchen was often located in the cellar along with rooms for storage. Typically, two bedrooms were located upstairs over the parlour and the dining room.

The array of modern services which we take for granted were largely non-existent in the Georgian terrace and we should generally be grateful that we cannot recapture the smells of the past. Whatever the architectural and aesthetic charms of Georgian proportions, joinery and plasterwork, its plumbing was crude, its sanitation primitive and its lighting and heating rather rudimentary. The bathroom as we know it—a separate room dedicated to our daily hygiene and ablutions—did not exist in the Georgian terrace. The lavatory was not located in or next to the bathroom but exiled to a small enclosure at the bottom of the backyard. Long before the appearance of the 'night soil' carters and connections to sewerage lines, the humble Georgian lavatory sat above a pit. Cooking was done in the kitchen on a wood-fired cast-iron stove. Cutlery, plates, pots and pans were washed up in timber sinks, often in the next room, the scullery. Without refrigeration, preserving food was difficult and most cooked meals were intended for immediate consumption.

## SURVIVING EXAMPLES

Georgian terrace houses are relatively rare in Australia and they were never built in the large numbers that characterise the later Victorian era. They are confined to New South Wales, mostly in and around Sydney, or scattered in the Tasmanian towns and cities, such as Launceston and Hobart. The earliest were very modest, often single-storey dwellings, sometimes with attic bedrooms. A surviving row of terraces in Paddington, Sydney, built in the 1840s to accommodate the stonemasons who built the Victoria Barracks nearby, clearly illustrates many of these characteristics.

## PLANNING THE GARDEN

The layout of early terrace house gardens in Australia reflected their English precursors. It was not until the eighteenth century in England that ownership of a small town garden became the expectation of an expanding urban middle class. The best surviving example is the Officers' Terrace at the Royal Naval Dockyard at Chatham in Kent, England. This terrace is all the more important because substantial documentary evidence, in the form of a model and detailed plans of the layout of the gardens dating from 1774, still exists. The accuracy of the plans, which are kept at the Map Library of the British Museum, was verified in the mid-1980s.

The success of the scheme relied on the twelve houses being planned and built as a whole, including both front and back gardens. The gardens, separated from the rear of the houses by a back carriageway, were walled and laid out symmetrically in perfect harmony with the architecture of the houses. Each garden had a central walk flanked by garden beds, the majority of which were slim rectangles of various sizes. The visitor could walk directly to the end of the garden to a covered seat or summerhouse with the option of returning either directly or by taking another path bordering the garden plot on its outer edge. One of the gardens boasted a more ornate scheme; it was set out in a circular arrangement with garden beds as the central feature.

The layout appears to have been designed for ease of cultivation, with the walls around each garden planted on three sides with espaliered fruit trees. A sweet bay (*Laurus nobilis*), believed to be a remnant of one of the back gardens, still stands in one of the courtyards, and fragments of trellis and covered walks survive.

There is little remaining to show how the early Georgian terraces of New South Wales and Tasmania were gardened, if they were gardened at all. By 1800 the most populated area of Sydney was The Rocks. The terrace houses of the era did not usually have front yards so gardening activity was confined to the back. The main emphasis for the gardens of this time was their usefulness. Contemporary advertisements stressed the presence of fruit trees, vegetable plots, fences and wells as essential adjuncts for a comfortable residence.

**ABOVE:** *Dianthus*, the most common among them the carnation, were popular flowers in the nineteenth-century terrace garden. *Dianthus* were among the many flowers that may have embellished early terrace house gardens as it was introduced into New South Wales as early as 1819.

**LEFT:** The original layout of this garden in a Sydney Georgian-style terrace house is unknown beyond the position of the pathway. Mature roses and hardy aspidistras survive, but the grassed area would need to be excavated to reveal any evidence remaining of the original beds, which may have been geometrically arranged. The show of old 'cape bulbs', such as watsonias, is evidence of how South African plants were collected by ships en route to the colony and made themselves at home.

**BELOW:** Choko vines, such as this one in the backyard of a Susannah Place terrace, were a popular choice in colonial Sydney.

**BELOW LEFT:** This illustration is of the plans for the Naval Officers' Terrace, Chatham, England, the best surviving example of eighteenth-century terrace garden layouts. English garden plans were the only models available to any early Australian gardener.

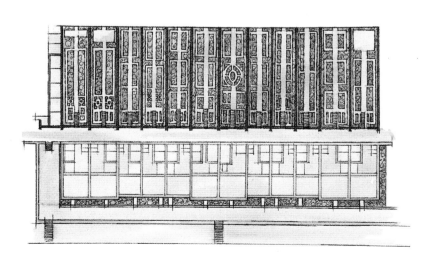

Many terrace houses built during the Regency period were essentially Georgian with a few more fashionably sophisticated details added. Jobbins Terrace, built c.1855 in Gloucester Street, The Rocks, falls into this category. Overall the details are typically Georgian—rubbed brickwork lintels over the windows and doors, flush six-paneled front doors and six-paned double-hung window sashes. The subtle, almost imperceptible breakfront of the façade and the elegant mouldings of the parapet cornice display a yearning for Regency elegance.

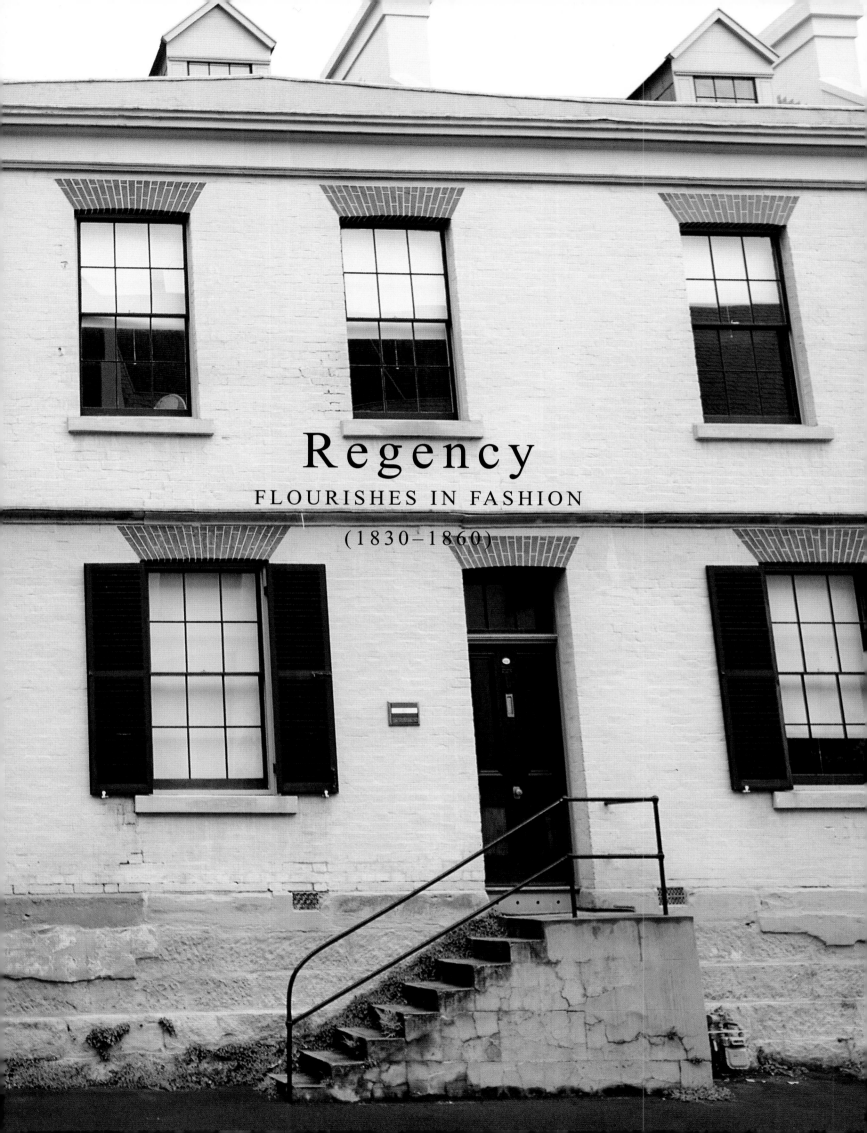

# Regency

## FLOURISHES IN FASHION

### (1830–1860)

The appearance of the Regency style in Australian architecture marks a highly significant phase in the cultural development of the young colonies for it signals the first attempt to be up-to-date with architectural fashion. Whereas the inspiration for Australian Georgian architecture derived socially and aesthetically from modest English provincialism, the patrons of the colonial Regency style aspired to emulate the prevailing architectural taste patronised by royalty and the fashionable upper classes in London.

LEFT: Decorative cast iron, such as this detail on a first-floor balcony c.1860, first appeared on terraces in the Regency period. The flat, pilaster-like verandah column, common in New South Wales though not elsewhere in Australia, became widely used in Victorian times.

In Australian architecture the Regency style was most successfully applied to domestically scaled residential buildings. It proved to be an ideal vehicle for the display of new-found wealth and success, constrained only by a reticent use of ornament and restraint from excessive or vulgar flashiness. Ironically, this was in sharp contrast to the greatest expression of the style, the Prince Regent's extraordinary Chinese/Mogul confection, John Nash's remodelling of the Royal Pavilion at Brighton in Sussex. Later generations, during the time of Victorian, Boom and Federation styles, embraced a similar sense of exuberance, revelling in showy displays of ornament or self-conscious prettiness and quaintness of detail.

Rather than the terrace house, we must look instead to the grand patrician suburban marine villas of Sydney Harbour, such as Elizabeth Bay House, or the dignified rural homesteads of northern Tasmania, such as 'Clarendon', in order to find the style's most eloquent expression. That the Regency style reached such a remarkable level of refinement and sophistication of design compared with its Georgian antecedents of two or three decades earlier is a remarkable achievement.

The Australian colonies had only recently passed their critical stage of survival and now entered a period of more mature economic and aesthetic development. While it is true that basic improvements to building construction and the prevention of water penetration occurred throughout the nineteenth century, the elegance and subtlety of the Regency detailing, especially its joinery, was never surpassed and rarely, if ever, equalled.

**ABOVE:** Of the original seven Regency terrace houses built in 1836, which made up Horbury Terrace in Sydney's Macquarie Street, only two, numbers 171 and 173, survive today. This engraving from Joseph Fowles' *Sydney in 1848* depicts a largely Georgian-influenced building with some smart Regency features.

**RIGHT:** Numbers 171 and 173 Macquarie Street are all that remain of Horbury Terrace. Despite the chaste architectural expression of the wall of the street façade, great subtlety and refinement is evident in the delicacy of the first-floor French doors and surviving internal joinery.

**LEFT:** The architecture of this terrace is Georgian in style but the garden is reminiscent of the Regency period when flower beds and garden ornaments became more popular. During the first half of the nineteenth century sundials, plinths, urns and fountains were either imported or carved from local sandstone. For reasons of cost, they generally graced only the gardens of the well-to-do. Cliveas, seen here growing in the shade of the pepper tree, survive in many older gardens. The heavily-glazed paving bricks became common in the latter half of the nineteenth century.

**LEFT:** Sadly, only the most modest of John Verge's terrace houses have survived the post-World War I boom. Numbers 39–41 Lower Fort Street in Millers Point, Sydney, were built in 1834 on the airy and healthy ridge above the dank squalor of The Rocks. The sunken basement accommodated the kitchen, scullery and cellar with the parlour and dining room above. Bedrooms were in the upper levels. By the most economical means, Verge used Francis Greenway's favoured device— borrowed from Sir John Soane—of emphasising window openings by pushing them into semi-circular headed, shallow recesses.

**BELOW LEFT:** The elegant anthemion motif of the cantilevered cast-iron balconies of Horbury Terrace distills the essence of English neo-classical detail worthy of the eighteenth-century Scottish architect Robert Adam.

**BELOW:** Regency architecture was readily identifiable by the sophisticated use of classical orders. The portico of 55 Lower Fort Street, Millers Point, uses Tuscan order on the columns and frieze in the correct architectural manner.

## EXOTIC TASTES

The Regency style took its name from the period and style in English architecture and the decorative arts which occurred during the political Regency of George, Prince of Wales (later George IV), from 1811 to 1820. In England, however, the style is generally considered to embrace the broader period 1790 to 1840 which had been clearly influenced by the Prince Regent. On its home turf it was a curious amalgam of restrained and exuberant elements. In its early days it was comprised of chaste neoclassicism but later Regency taste was successively overlaid with a growing interest in exotic styles drawn from Ancient Egypt, China and Mogul India as well as the rediscovery of Gothic medievalism. In Australia, Regency architecture was more modest. It flirted occasionally with Egyptian, rarely Chinese and not at all with Indian styles. On a few occasions, as in the design of villas such as 'Lindesay' at Darling Point in Sydney, it lightly embraced Gothic. Sadly, however, the design of Regency terrace houses reflected none of these more florid styles but drew inspiration instead from the classical influences of the Georgian house.

As a stylistic term for Australian architecture 'Regency' has been applied loosely by some historians. Although its legacy lingered on throughout Australia in certain identifiable forms almost to the end of the nineteenth century, the heyday of the Regency terrace was the 1830s, with diminishing frequency in the following two decades, and principally in New South Wales and Tasmania. Due to constraints of scale, setting or budget, the Regency terrace house presented no opportunity to dally in exotic stylistic characteristics. In architectural terms it merely overlaid the essential Georgian terrace house with more overt borrowings from classical architecture.

No other artist has captured the seductive qualities of early Australian Georgian and Regency architecture in quite the same way as William Hardy Wilson did in his *Old Colonial Architecture in New South Wales and Tasmania*. This detail depicts a house in Gloucester Street, The Rocks, long since demolished to make way for the Sydney Harbour Bridge approaches. Louvred shutters appeared in Georgian buildings, but the French doors with margin bars and cast-iron balustrade, similar to Horbury Terrace, are typical of the Regency flavour in Australia.

When it was built in 1833, The Colonnade, designed by John Verge, boasted the smartest shops in Sydney with 'commodious residences' in the upper levels. Verge made a virtue of the sloping site in Bridge Street by stepping a colonnaded Tuscan verandah down the hill. The shallow breakfront of the central bay is borrowed from Chippendale's bookcases of two generations earlier.

## INSPIRATION AND IMITATION

Most Regency architecture, whether in England or Australia, expended much effort in pretending it was something else. In England that might have been a Mogul Indian palace or a Chinese temple. In Australia the deception, less fanciful and more modest, usually tried to pass off a cheap material for a more expensive one. This is evident in the treatment of the external walls where smooth lime plaster, applied over brickwork, was ruled out in lines to simulate good quality ashlar. Generally the proportions followed those of Georgian houses, where symmetry was a basic rule.

Modelling of the building profile, refinement of details and the elimination of awkward elements, differentiate the Regency terrace from its Georgian forebears. Such concerns are evident in the replacement of the practical, if sometimes heavy, overhanging roof eaves with a concealed gutter behind an upstanding parapet, creating a vertical continuation of the wall surface above the roof line. Parapets allowed for the addition of architectural mouldings and other decoration which related the house more directly to its ultimate source of inspiration, the classical temple. The obvious advantage in the use of this architectural device was that the top of the façade could be fully developed, decorated and terminated, independent of the roof form. In practice, however, locating a box gutter out of sight and sitting over the front often led to serious water damage in the event of failure. In more elaborate terraces windows and doorways, like the parapet, were sometimes decorated with projecting mouldings and brackets to delineate the proportions.

## VERANDAHS AND BALCONIES

The most important advance in the design of the Regency terrace lay not in its higher level of sophistication in architectural detailing, but in grafting the verandah from the freestanding house and cottage

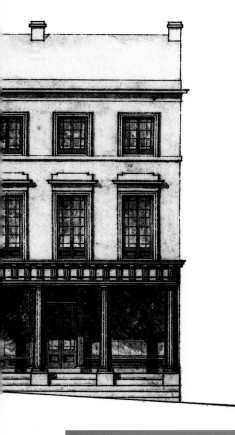

**ABOVE:** This detail from William Hardy Wilson's *Old Colonial Architecture in New South Wales and Tasmania* shows the double Ionic portico of 20–22 Lower Fort Street, The Rocks, in Sydney. The names applied to the buildings, 'Euripedes' and 'Sophocles', existed only in William Hardy Wilson's romanticised drawing, they did not appear on the buildings.

**LEFT:** 20–22 Lower Fort Street is one of the finest examples of Sydney's few surviving Regency terraces. A wide array of architectural treatments has been used to excellent effect on the buildings: the ground-floor stucco strikes a bold note with horizontal rustication; the pair of fine cantilevered cast-iron balconies open from three pairs of French doors; and the bedrooms on the second floor have smaller, though well-proportioned, windows befitting their function.

The terraces that make up 57–61 Lower Fort Street resemble London townhouses built by Thomas Cubitt to the north and south of Hyde Park during the early Victorian era. A rusticated ground floor provides a strong visual base to the smooth plastered walls above. String courses, bracketed lintel mouldings and a strong projecting cornice at the parapet add refined Regency touches.

onto the terrace-house form. This was a more complex process than it might at first appear. Whereas house or cottage verandahs usually wrapped around three sides, the terrace house offered only its principal or street façade. The terrace house verandah, after making its appearance in the 1830s, was quickly absorbed into the archetype and later became an essential part of the image of the typical nineteenth-century terrace house.

Unlike those of Georgian houses, the earliest verandahs on Regency terraces were usually cantilevered or projected out from the first floor without the support of columns or posts. The cantilevered balcony relied on the principle of give and take. As most Regency terraces were built right up to the street alignment, the cantilevered balcony allowed the 'borrowing' of a little of the public domain whilst returning a common benefit of shelter from rain and sun. Innumerable examples can be seen in Joseph

Fowles's elegant drawings of Sydney streets which appeared in his *Sydney in 1848*. With the verandah appeared a new material in the architectural vocabulary of the terrace house: ornamental cast iron. This, more than any other building material, came to define the essential character of the Australian terrace house.

In terms of creature comforts the Regency terrace house differed little from its Georgian predecessor. Cooking and bathing arrangements remained largely as before: plumbing, drainage and sewerage were at best rudimentary and sometimes non-existent. Only in the grandest Regency mansions and villas did a separate room, the forerunner of the modern bathroom, make its appearance. As before, the ground-floor room facing the street was almost always the parlour with the dining room behind it. If there was no basement, the kitchen was usually placed immediately behind the dining room with a small yard beyond.

LYON'S TERRACE          HYDE PARK.

**ABOVE:** Completed in 1841, Lyon's Terrace was the grandest and finest Regency terrace built in Australia. It stood in Liverpool Street and looked down imperiously on the southern end of Hyde Park. Joseph Fowles, whose engraving is shown here, thought they would have suited London's Regent's Park well. Built several years after John Verge's retirement, it is speculated that Verge's assistant, John Bibb, was the designer. If so, he clearly outdid his master.

**ABOVE:** Melbourne boasts a number of early Victorian terraces that carry on the Regency style, even if a little coarsely. These two terraces in Lygon Street, Fitzroy, erected in 1861–62, incorporate the rusticated ground-floor loggia or colonnade, a device common in Melbourne but rare in Sydney. The bold mouldings around the windows and a deeply bracketed cornice betray heavy-handed Victorian style absent from the chaste elegance of Regency.

**RIGHT:** Now home to the Royal College of Physicians, 145 Macquarie Street, Sydney, was a two-storey townhouse when built in 1848. The two upper floors, added in 1910, closely match the earlier work. Most notable on the exterior is the splendid verandahs with finely cast Ionic columns. Behind the shutters sit Regency French doors with tell-tale margin bars. In recent years the building has undergone skilled conservation under the direction of Hector Abrahams of Clive Lucas Stapleton and Partners.

*Utricularia intermedia.*

*Fuchsia globòsa.*

*Verónica hybrida.*

**ABOVE:** *The Floricultural Cabinet and Florist's Magazine* was one of a number of British publications devoted to gardening or botany, providing inspiration during the Regency period. *Fuchsia globosa* (centre), now known as *Fuchsia magellanica* cv. Globosa, was popular in Sydney at the time, unlike the uncommon milfoil or *Urticularia intermedia* (left), a native of Britain. *Veronica hybrida* (right) was less common but featured in William Macarthur's *Catalogue of Plants Cultivated at Camden Park, NSW* in 1857.

**RIGHT:** William Hardy Wilson's talents were displayed at their most seductive when he captured dappled light and shade. Richmond Terrace, long since demolished but captured in *Old Colonial Architecture in New South Wales and Tasmania*, once overlooked Sydney's Domain. This reticent though commanding row represented the sober dignity characteristic of the Regency style in Sydney's grander terrace houses.

## REGENCY PRIVACY AND FLOWERS

Town planning in England during the Regency period was characterised by laying out streets and crescents with villa or terrace-house allotments centring on a garden square or 'subscription' garden. Increasingly, however, privacy rather than prospect was becoming valued by residents. The front garden, open to the street, displayed the respectability, propriety and taste of the occupants, whereas the back garden was for the privacy and personal use by the residents.

In Australia there are few examples of the concept of terrace houses surrounding a garden square, and those that were built, such as the terraces of St Vincent Place in Melbourne, generally occurred later. Local resident Anabella Boswell recalled her impressions of the grand gardens of the government officials whose houses faced Macquarie Place in Sydney in a journal in the mid-1830s. She writes of pretty front gardens and verandahs sheltered by climbing roses and other flowering plants.

These were the gardens of the elite of the colony but her description and those of other writers of the time confirms that by this stage there was little to choose between the way town gardens were laid out in Sydney and those in the suburbs of London. The major difference appears to have been the 'large luxuriant masses of geraniums (*Pelargonium*) and roses'. Banksias and China roses were popular choices for the New South Wales climate. In addition, the gardens of Sydney boasted fruit trees, such as orange and lemon, which were far too delicate for the English climate.

# Early Victorian

## AN ELEGANT ERA
### (1850–1870)

The ascent of Queen Victoria to the throne in 1837 brought no immediate change to architectural taste in England or in the colonies. By 1850, however, new and discernible stylistic traits in architecture had begun to emerge, heralding the rise of a greatly enlarged middle class, newly enriched by the fruits of the Industrial Revolution. With their wealth came a new and growing market for architecture and decorative objects. Despite the pioneering role that Britain played in industrial and manufacturing development, in matters of taste and aesthetics English designers and architects suffered a profound crisis, finding great difficulty in applying their skills to new building materials and processes. Instead of attempting to create an architectural style that 'spoke the language of its time', more than ever before architects and designers preferred to look back to what they saw as the comforting historical styles of the past. Australian architects and building designers followed faithfully, although a few steps behind.

The tradition of drawing from historic precedents was, of course, well established. Builders of Georgian terraces in Australia relied upon well-tested and accepted principles derived from classical architecture adapted from British habits and modified to meet Australian needs. Local Regency builders added some spare architectural trim but generally did not venture down the byways of stylistic exoticism favoured by their more flamboyant English cousins.

**ABOVE:** The allotment side boundaries of the Hoddle Street terraces in Paddington, Sydney, strike the street at an acute angle. Such irregularities were the result of street subdivisions following boundaries of original land grants of larger estates. The stepped terrace frontages provide a visually complex and satisfying streetscape, and the recently planted clipped hedges are sympathetic to the unusual architecture of the houses.

**BELOW:** It was common for terrace houses to comprise three or four levels. The basement, hidden from sight, was often built on the hilly slopes of Sydney, but rarely seen in the flatter topography of Melbourne, Adelaide, Perth or Fremantle. On the ground floor were the parlour, dining room and kitchen (if not in the basement) and on the upper levels the bedrooms.

**PREVIOUS PAGES LEFT:** Dormers were common to freestanding as well as terrace houses and have an ancient lineage dating from medieval times or earlier. The decorative barge boards and spiky turned finial of this early Victorian terrace in Davenport Street, Hobart, demonstrate how functional building elements were readily dressed up in architectural clothes.

**PREVIOUS PAGES RIGHT:** During the Victorian era, improved technology and production techniques led to increased diversity in building materials and decorative finishes; enough to satisfy demand for rich colour and pattern. The sobriety of the black and white, marble, checkerboard verandah floor tiling of this modest early Victorian terrace in Ivy Street near Sydney University is challenged by highly coloured, transfer-patterned ceramic tiles applied to the riser of the front door threshold.

LEFT: This photograph was taken c.1890. Before the advent of cantilevered awnings, shops and pubs protected their clientele from the weather with deep verandah roofs. The concave roof was intended to recall the striped canvas awnings used in earlier times and was often painted with wide stripes in cream and Brunswick green or Indian red. The durable and decorative timber picket fence, also shown here, was a cheaper alternative to wrought iron palisade fencing.

RIGHT: Hobart, like Sydney, was blessed with topographical features which challenged the ingenuity of the terrace house builder. This group of houses which tumble down Davenport Street are an eloquent demonstration of the terrace house's ability to adapt to any terrain, no matter how hilly.

LEFT: The use of contrasting light and dark brickwork was more popular in Melbourne than other Australian towns. In this terrace in Carlton a simple flower garden fills the area between the verandah and the street.

The use of applied lime stucco or cement render over brickwork, first introduced in the Regency terrace house as a vehicle for high-style architectural detailing, was embraced with enthusiasm in the era of the early Victorian terrace house. As before, the use of stucco with ruled lines pretending to be expensive stonemasonry was an artifice to give the impression of fine and expensive materials when a modest purse was paying the bills. Impressing passers-by through deception was only one advantage of the rendered wall; another more practical advantage was the improved waterproofing it provided.

Generally, flat expanses of wall were left as an undecorated face except for the discreet pattern of simulated fine joints. It was around doorways and windows, and in the parapets and chimneys that the stucco craftsmen's art found an opportunity for creative expression. In these places the otherwise two-dimensional quality of the houses' façades could be readily layered and plastered with rich detail such as mouldings, string courses, console brackets, modillions, swags and urns. The sharp shadows cast in the Australian sun gave houses a great sense of depth and detail.

Colour also played a fundamental role. Contrast between the smooth, flat planes of the walls and the richly modelled decoration formed the basis of almost all colour schemes. Popular wall colours followed closely those of natural earth or stone: rich creams, umbers, siennas, light and dark browns, even deep Indian reds. Depending upon the depth of the wall colour the stucco trim was generally painted in boldly contrasting colours, whether lighter or darker.

## DECORATIVE IRON LACE

No other building material characterised the Victorian terrace house so completely and so distinctively as decorative cast iron. Often this material has been popularly called 'iron lace' or even 'Sydney lace' and has prompted some architectural historians to invent a new stylistic term to herald its use, 'Victorian filigree'. Cast iron was applied predominantly to the verandahs of the Victorian terrace house to form the verandah posts, decorative brackets, friezes and valances. Combined with wrought iron, it was also widely used for the

**LEFT:** The corner shop of Susannah Place has been recreated by the New South Wales Historic Houses Trust to resemble a general grocer's store from the early twentieth century. A typical Victorian store would not have looked very different from this one, except that it might have been more fully stocked.

**BELOW:** Dating terraces on the basis of the stylistic characteristics is problematic and often misleading. The row at 68–80 Mary Anne Street, Ultimo, Sydney, was built between 1869–70, just before the advent of the Boom style, yet the houses display a decidedly old-fashioned taste for Georgian rubbed brick lintels over the windows and six-panel front doors. In 1994 extensive conservation work was undertaken by Peter Todd of Design 5 Architects in association with Allen Jack + Cottier.

**LEFT:** The typical Victorian grocery shop window changed relatively little over time, though the sizes of the panes gradually increased and glazing bars, such as these at 64 Susannah Place, eventually disappeared.

Often, in Victorian streetscapes, a curious sense of harmony was created out of the very diversity of styles. Sometimes the houses were extremely different in character, height and alignment as can be seen in this photograph (c.1885) of a street identified only as Railway Place, somewhere in New South Wales. Ironically, most states today have planning laws which would forbid these sorts of irregular terrace house forms and alignments.

decorative elements of palisade fences and gates, such as gate posts or finials. In grander houses it was sometimes used to achieve a delicate silhouette against the sky when applied as cresting along the roof ridge. The earliest cast iron was imported from Britain as ships' ballast but from the 1840s it was manufactured in most Australian cities and major towns. The number and diversity of patterns grew as the century progressed.

The earliest surviving decorative cast iron, found in New South Wales and Tasmania, dates generally from the 1830s. An excellent example can be seen in the two remnant terraces of the Horbury Terrace in Sydney's Macquarie Street. Joseph Fowles's *Sydney in 1848* records Horbury Terrace as a row of seven Regency terraces stretching north from the corner of Bent Street. Here each of the first-floor windows opened onto shallow, individual, cantilevered balconies, just large enough to hold one or two people. These rather tentative Regency balconies were soon replaced in the Victorian era by deeper full-width projecting verandahs.

Over time, the plan of the typical Victorian terrace underwent small but significant changes. The most important of these was the development of the service or kitchen wing. As we have noted, the earliest terrace houses tended to have the kitchen located in the basement, or even detached from the house itself. By the middle of the nineteenth century the kitchen was usually located in a wing built out from the back of the main structure, about half the width of the building allotment. Beyond the kitchen, and often attached to the back of it, was the laundry open on one or two sides. Where a second storey was built over the kitchen wing, the rooms most often included were one or more small bedrooms, and sometimes a bathroom. The lavatory remained in exile at the bottom of the backyard, close to the back lane and convenient to the night soil cart.

## LET THERE BE LIGHT

New or improved materials inevitably played an important role in all forms of architecture. Improvements in the manufacture of glass, especially the appearance of plate glass in the 1850s and 1860s, substantially altered the design of the double-hung, vertically sliding timber sash window. The Georgian and Regency practice of dividing each window sash into six or more separate panes, each approximating the 'golden section' (the division of a line in a ratio of three to five, regarded as an ideal division), was dictated by the limits to the size of panes that could be produced rather than any slavish adherence to ideals of classical proportions. As the pane sizes increased, in dimensions as well as in cost, the need for glazing bars disappeared.

At first the sashes tended to be glazed with two panes divided by a vertical glazing bar. Later each sash contained a single pane, dispensing with the need for a glazing bar. The corners of Georgian and Regency sashes finished with a clean right angle, the network of glazing bars providing substantial internal structural bracing to the sash frame.

The disappearance of the glazing bar in the Victorian window, however, presented the maker of a single-paned window sash with the problem of weakened joints at the corners, usually the lower corners of the top sash and the

**ABOVE:** Falconer Terrace in Napier Street, Fitzroy, Melbourne, was built between 1866 and 1884. The eight houses are made of rendered brick and bluestone, a local stone, and feature an arcaded colonnade with shallow arched heads set flush to the front wall, an element favoured in Melbourne architecture.

**LEFT:** Melbourne followed fashions and ideas from Britain, Europe and North America with a seriousness and intellectual hauteur not matched elsewhere in Australia. Built in 1889–94, the nine Paterson Street terraces in Carlton North use polychrome brickwork, a material introduced to Melbourne during the 1860–70s through the influence of John Ruskin's writings and the English Gothic Revival architect George Edmund Street.

upper corners of the bottom sash. To overcome this a 'horn' or vertical member of the sash frame was extended to give greater strength and rigidity. The horn was subsequently cut in a variety of patterns to transform a purely functional device into a decorative element. It was quite common in this period for the less important window sashes at the rear of the house to be made up of six panes for reasons of economy.

The restrained simplicity of Regency plasterwork and joinery gave way in Victorian times to heavier, more deeply modelled details. These changes can best be seen in the proportions and details of the staircase, where the newel post emerged as a major decorative element. The earlier slenderness of the handrail and balusters was gradually replaced with coarser sections with more elaborate, 'meatier' turned profiles. Parallel trends can also readily be seen in the detailing of joinery elements such as skirtings, architraves and chimneypieces, and in the plasterwork of cornices and ceiling rosettes.

## ECONOMY AND STYLE IN THE GARDEN

In 1838 the Scottish gardening writer John Claudius Loudon put forward some ideas on garden design for a wide range of houses in his book *The Suburban Gardener and Villa Companion*. Loudon did not use the term 'terrace house' but referred to them as 'houses in a connected row with seldom much depth at the front for a garden'. 'It must be obvious' he added, 'that in gardens of so regular a shape, whether large or small, there can be very little variety produced in laying them out; that the style adopted must be regular, as indicated by the shape and the boundaries of the house; and that the chief interest must depend on the trees and plants introduced and their culture'.

Loudon was aware of cost constraints in the establishment of the gardens of such dwellings. For a shady front garden he recommended a grass plot with a single evergreen shrub such as laurustinus (*Viburnum tinus*), aucuba, box, or variegated holly. Additional shrubs could be introduced if the situation was sunny with one or more deciduous or evergreen flowering shrubs in the centre of the plot. Suggestions for this centre group included arbutus, Persian lilac and red flowering currant (*Ribes sanguineum*). Against the walls, Loudon proposed common honeysuckle, Virginia creeper, common ivy, white and purple clematis, Ayrshire rose, Boursault rose, or a Noisette rose.

Deep front gardens were more common in Victorian-style terraces in Melbourne than Sydney. This long row in Collins Street, Surry Hills, Sydney, was built in 1875. It represents mid-Victorian design with minimal ornamentation. Hedges of privet, tecomaria and viburnum were popular for those who wanted to keep their gardens simple. Murraya is often substituted for privet by today's gardeners.

**LEFT:** A centrally placed sundial within a simple circular bed surrounded by a gravel path and flower beds is a garden layout chosen by many terrace house owners. The garden at this East Melbourne home is one of many where a geometric scheme was used following the recommendations of nineteenth-century garden authors.

**LEFT:** Before the advent of large sheets of glass, the design of the window sash in double-hung windows required the use of a central glazing bar. A skilled joiner created the half-round heads of the upper sash in this window.

**BELOW:** The garden of this terrace follows the principle of using a centrally placed shrub as the major feature. In Sydney this was often a gardenia or camellia bush. The back garden is divided from the front by latticed screens, separating the public and private gardened spaces.

**BELOW:** Many people think French doors and French windows are the same. The French window, seen here, is a double-hung window reaching to the floor. Unlike French doors, they are not easy to use as the unwary will attest from minor head injuries.

## FLORAL PATTERNS

An alternative to planting shrubs, Loudon suggested, was a circular bed dug approximately one metre in diameter with a central evergreen flowering plant such as *Saxifraga crassifolia* (now known as *Bergenia crassifolia*) which could be bordered with annuals such as mignonette, candytuft or nemophilia. For those primarily interested in a floral display, he suggested surrounding the front garden with a border with a small geometric bed, or beds, in the centre.

The back garden was to be laid out simply with a walkway around the edge and provision at the bottom for a clothesline and garden refuse pit or compost bin. The walls could be covered with ornamental plants or espaliered fruit trees. A long list of suggested shrubs and small trees was included—many beyond the scope of the gardens attached to the tiny Victorian terraces which were to be built in the larger Australian cities. This scheme was essentially for an ornamental garden. Another option was to give the backyard over to a functional kitchen garden with vegetables and fruit trees.

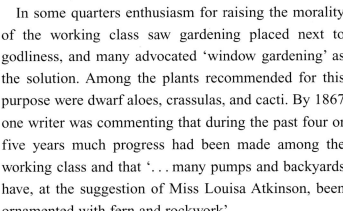

Edward Kemp, in the third edition of his book *How to Lay Out a Garden* (1865), recommended that the front gardens of attached rows of houses be made common to all, or that they at least be planned in such a way as to complement each other, preferably with only light wire fences dividing each garden from its neighbours. Both Loudon's and Kemp's publications were read by many in Australia and a few of their suggestions for geometrically shaped garden beds were adopted by villa, cottage and terrace-house owners. Surrounded by gravel, these beds were often edged with box, thrift, thyme, parsley or strawberries. Alternatively, they could be edged with bricks, slates or terracotta tiles which, in Sydney, were being manufactured for gardens by 1864.

It remains a sad fact that the back gardens of many terrace houses appear to have been neglected, characterised simply by the ubiquitous and essential outside lavatory situated near the back lane with the remaining area, if the space was small, used only for clothes drying. From the mid-1860s members of the Sydney Horticultural Society attempted to raise the public's consciousness of this horticultural oversight in publications which provided positive descriptions and suggestions. Mr Pennington of Bligh Street received praise for his neat, commodious greenhouse filled with ferns and begonias. In the front windows of his house he had placed Wardian cases, similar to miniature greenhouses, stocked with ferns. The writer commented that the staghorn could be fastened to walls and suggested a bird's nest fern for the shady side of a yard. Alderman Broomfield's garden in Pyrmont was a typical width of approximately twenty feet (six metres), with a straight path running directly through its centre. The upper section of the garden consisted of beds divided by cement walks and contained plants, such as carnations, roses, fuchsias, pansies, pelargonium, gladioli and verbenas. The inventive Alderman watered this via a hose attached to the bathroom. In the lower part of the garden, where not a weed was in sight, grew a variety of dahlias.

In some quarters enthusiasm for raising the morality of the working class saw gardening placed next to godliness, and many advocated 'window gardening' as the solution. Among the plants recommended for this purpose were dwarf aloes, crassulas, and cacti. By 1867 one writer was commenting that during the past four or five years much progress had been made among the working class and that '... many pumps and backyards have, at the suggestion of Miss Louisa Atkinson, been ornamented with fern and rockwork'.

**ABOVE:** Arum lily, *Zantedeschia aethipica*, thrives in moist positions. It was first introduced into Australia in the 1820s and was a popular plant in the eastern states, even considered a luxuriant element in Victorian gardens, but became a weed in many areas of Western Australia.

LEFT: This backyard in The Rocks, Sydney, c.1900, features a garden of ferns and shells, both widely used as ornaments throughout the nineteenth century. Gardening efforts during this time did little to alleviate the dismal reality of terrace house living in many inner Sydney areas.

ABOVE: Doing the laundry was difficult in the Victorian terrace. Few wood-fired laundry 'coppers' survive intact in terrace houses to show us the sheer drudgery of household work. This one at Susannah Place in The Rocks is a reminder of this unromantic aspect of the past.

RIGHT: Street trees can provide a warm garden atmosphere for many terraces which extend below street level and have limited space for individual gardens.

**ABOVE:** Cast and deeply moulded applied stucco ornaments were a hallmark of the Boom-style terrace. Party fire walls afforded prominent positions to embellish with architectural ornaments, stylised plant forms or even human profiles. The romantic imagery of roses adds to the ornamentation of the grander terraces of this era.

**RIGHT:** Dorset Terrace in St Vincent Place, South Melbourne, built in 1872, represents Boom-style urbanity at its best. Exceptionally wide terraces set in deep front gardens, richly stuccoed walls and elaborate decorative cast iron have been blended together to form a row of Boom-style terraces that represent the heady success of 'Marvellous Melbourne'. Smartly tiled garden paths, bordered with neat flower beds, allow an impression of a large front garden shared by the residents of Dorset Terrace.

# Boom Style

## ITALIANATE FASHIONS

(1870–1890)

**ABOVE LEFT:** The conspicuous display of wealth underlay all aspects of Boom-style houses. The exterior walls provided the greatest canvas for overblown decoration. The central parapet of Tasma Terrace in Parliament Place, Melbourne, exemplifies stucco elaboration.

**ABOVE RIGHT:** The uninhibited exuberance of the stuccoer's skill is best seen in the parapets and entablatures of Melbourne's Boom-style terraces. In Brunswick Street, Fitzroy, a rich segmental pediment caps the parapet with a triumphant flourish.

The boom and bust cycle of the Australian economy is not a recent phenomenon. From the early days of colonial settlement Australia's financial well-being was dependent upon the fluctuating export value of agricultural products and on the economies of countries beyond our shores. While recessions and depressions have the effect of slowing down building activity or bringing it to a virtual standstill, the boom periods unleash tidal waves of development that, generation after generation, renew, transform and, more recently, disfigure our towns and cities.

The economic boom that followed the gold rushes of the 1850s and 1860s was centred on the large Australian towns and cities, and it was built largely on the shaky foundation of land speculation which was propped up by unscrupulous business practices. This led to a unique situation in our architectural history, the economic buoyancy of the 1870s and 1880s left its name in our stylistic lexicon as the 'Boom style'.

## MARVELLOUS MELBOURNE

Although the Boom style found expression in all major towns, it was in the capital cities, the honey pots for the nouveau riche bees, that its architectural legacy was most evident, most concentrated and most ostentatious. In 'Marvellous Melbourne' the Boom style reached its most flamboyant heights with the building of Australia's most lavishly decorated mansions and grandest terrace houses. Not since the time of John Verge's commodious Regency rows in Sydney had the terrace been treated as accommodation for the rich and fashionable. The Boom style developed as a highly embellished form of the Italianate style, an English architectural fashion of the nineteenth century drawn from a discovery of the irregular rural villa romantically located within an idealised Italian landscape. Irregularity of plan, massing and form combined with picturesque silhouettes comprised of belvedere towers, broken roof lines and clustered chimneys marked the readily identifiable characteristics of the larger Italianate houses and villas in Australia. But direct connections between the expression of Italianate style in Australia and its Italian origins were virtually non-existent.

Historians Richard Apperly, Robert Irving and Peter Reynolds in *Identifying Australian Architecture* have observed that its '. . . prominent characteristics—the faceted bay and stilted arch—were not specifically Italian at all'. Other stylistic flavours were sometimes overlaid if the budget matched the social pretensions: a hint of French Second Empire might emerge in the roof line, a touch of the Romanesque might embrace the tower or a flush of Tudor might erupt in the gable ends.

The Boom-style terrace house, however, rarely had the flexibility to express the extensive range of picturesque elements or stylistic cocktails that were frequently used in large, freestanding mansions. Richness of ornament and inflation of scale are the predominant elements, which distinguish the Boom-style terrace from its Victorian forebears.

## STUCCO EMBELLISHMENTS

No other Australian city could match the scale and architectural pretension of the best Melbourne Boom-style houses. Here the stuccoers' art had its greatest expression in the exuberant decoration applied to front façades, party walls and, especially, parapets. The purpose of stucco had remained the same since the days of the Regency terrace—to simulate traditional stonemasonry and its rich array of carved decoration, surface textures and finishes. The lower reaches of the wall surfaces, below roof level, provided rich opportunities for decorative embellishment with the application of deeply modelled mouldings, pilasters, human masks, and so on. A wide variety of textured or modelled wall finishes was possible in the hands of the

The six houses of Tasma Terrace in Parliament Place are among the grandest to survive in Melbourne's city centre. Designed by architect Charles Webb and built in 1878–87 each house comprises three storeys set off the ground to give a level base to a sloping site. On the lower two floors are elaborate, arcaded cast-iron balconies, each three bays wide. The second-floor windows reflect the tripartite arrangement of the iron below and the top of the parapet is terminated by a vigorously modelled stuccoed balustrade. Tasma Terrace is now the headquarters of Victoria's National Trust.

skilled stuccoer. Architectural emphasis was often achieved at the base of the terrace, at corners or around openings such as doorways and windows, by the use of quoins, which simulated slightly raised blocks of ashlar masonry, each piece alternating large and small size. At the ground level base courses were used and, in places where emphasis was required, other similar forms of applied surface texture were popular. Sometimes rustication was used to give the impression of rough-hewn stonework. More highly worked visual effects were achieved by the use of vermiculation, a texture which gave the appearance of the stonework having been eaten away by worms. For effect, these textures would sometimes be applied to the quoin stones. But the greatest expressions of elaborate stucco decoration were most often reserved for the parapet where the modelling became deeper and more extravagant. With the added drama of a silhouette against the sky, parapets allowed the imaginative craftsman a virtual blank cheque.

Among the array of decorative devices used were urns, finials, balustrades both pierced and blind, swags of fruit and flowers, projecting consoles and brackets, modillions and paterae. In some especially choice

**LEFT:** The hallway of 10 Tasma Terrace embraces the visitor with the gentle force of a volcanic eruption: painted, gilded, waxed and polished surfaces and textures all scream for attention and capture the quintessence of fast money and flashy taste. Only the gambling casinos of our own time match the flamboyance and vivacity of Boom-style interior decoration.

**BELOW:** Deep, intricately moulded plaster cornices provided the Boom-style decorator with a wonderful palette for mixing the boldness of strong colours with richly patterned frieze papers.

**BELOW:** Even the apparently humble and utilitarian ceramic tile was brilliantly exploited as a small canvas for highly coloured designs and patterns. This example, depicting lilliums and stylised sunflowers is from Newtown, Sydney, and was located in vertical panels between the front windows.

Rochester Terrace at St Vincent Place in Melbourne is beyond question the grandest Boom-style row in Australia. Set facing an extensive public garden in the manner of a traditional London square, it is one of the few terrace rows in Australia which use parkland as a major feature. Rochester Terrace was built by developer W. P. Buckhurst in the decade from 1869 on a scale that rivalled London's Regent's Park terraces, built by John Nash for the Prince Regent.

examples clam shells 'explode' from the wall. Where a row of terraces, or even a single house, needed to proclaim its name or date, moulded panels, escutcheons and heraldic shields were used to great effect.

Decorative cast iron was applied to the verandahs and balconies with a similar enthusiasm for richness. No longer was cast iron used merely as structural verandah posts and decorative balustrades, brackets and valances. It was increasingly applied as elaborate frieze panels, and was often used as highly ornate gate and fence posts, or even as delicate cresting along the main roof ridge. The decorative treatment of the cast itself became more elaborate and began to rival if not match that of the stucco. The quest for richer decorative treatment is perhaps best seen in the development of the balustrade, which in earlier eras was traditionally cast as a flat panel. With the increasing sophistication of modelling

and casting techniques it became possible in this era to produce panels with sinuous, baroque profiles.

## GARDENS, VERANDAHS AND PATHWAYS

By the 1870s, with the terrace as the preferred form of housing in urban areas, ambitious gardeners were becoming increasingly innovative in their treatment of confined spaces. In Glebe Point Road, Sydney, one householder turned verandah gardening into a fine art: overlooking three or four shelves of pot plants, the end wall of the verandah was painted with a landscape scene and the garden also included an ornamental wire fence and rockwork planted with ferns. In Woolloomooloo, Sydney, one verandah boasted a pyramid of stout wooden supports in a large tub and covered with *Ficus pumila* with an impressive specimen of cereus growing from the top. Rockwork embellished the base of the tub.

**ABOVE:** This detail of the entablature of Rochester Terrace shows the richly decorated stucco that was highly favoured during this era of architecture.

**RIGHT:** Identified as *Maranta illustris* in the 1870 publication *New and Rare Beautiful-Leaved Plant*s, but currently known as a species of *calathea*, this plant was collected from the Amazon region of Brazil and was well-suited for cultivation as a pot plant.

**BELOW:** The Italianate Boom-style house often embraced architectural details from disparate and even unrelated periods. The fretted barge boards of this grand terrace in Warren Ball Avenue in Sydney's Newtown are clearly Gothic in origin. Today camellias are the major planting in the front garden, but it is likely that more of the garden was given over to flower beds when the terrace was first built. The underplantings in the current garden are of clipped murraya and box.

BELOW: The composition of terraces in Walker Street in Lavender Bay, Sydney, displays an imaginative sense of design seldom found in Boom-style terraces. Because of the gentle slope, the street wall of each house has picturesque elements thrusting up or jutting out. Although highly decorated and impressive, Boom-style terraces allowed little space for a garden.

ABOVE: Intricate illustrations of fine-foliaged plants, such as this one reproduced in *New and Rare Beautiful-Leaved Plants*, provided the discerning verandah gardener with sources of inspiration.

RIGHT: Milton Terrace in Lower Fort Street, Millers Point, Sydney, sits in the shadow of the Sydney Harbour Bridge. Rising four storeys from semi-sunken basements, it rivals Melbourne's best in size but not in external decor. Some of the grandeur of Milton Terrace has been compromised by the enclosure of the first-floor balconies.

**RIGHT:** This unusual composition is the result of the allotment boundary striking the street at a very sharp angle. The row of five houses have been stepped back deeply from each other, and the picturesque shapes created are heightened by the protruding bay window on each house.

**BELOW:** This row of terraces in The Avenue in Randwick represents one of Sydney's grandest examples of Boom-style terraces. The central bay, which breaks forward and is carried up to a pediment at parapet level, is based on the Belvedere towers used to embellish grand Italianate mansions.

Many of the highly ornamented terraces of the boom years of the 1880s were large houses built to display the affluence or social pretensions of their occupants, but often with little space allowed for a garden. The layout of the front gardens differed very little from the recommendations made by Loudon fifty years earlier. Beyond the ornate iron gate set in palisade fencing the encaustic (coloured) tiled path generally led directly from the street to the front door. The garden was often to one side, its geometric layout edged with terracotta tiles, either plain or glazed, in one of the increasingly broad range of patterns available. Where the path bisected the garden the most popular choice was symmetrically placed circular beds. During this period it became common to see decorative urns, or vases as they were known, placed either on pedestals or at the end of a set of stairs.

Few intact examples of nineteenth-century terrace house gardens survive. However, Peter Watts in his book *Historic Gardens of Victoria* notes that despite the lack of surviving gardens it is evident that there was a wide variety of designs for such a small a patch of soil. Apart from the circle, the most common form, more complicated patterns in the shape of stars, crescents and scalloped edges were also used.

In 1885 an even more elaborate pattern was used for the garden of Daniel O'Connor's new residence, 'Tara' in Cleveland Street, Redfern. O'Connor had recently been appointed postmaster-general for New South Wales. A garden designed to complement the new house, a large freestanding terrace house with views

overlooking Prince Alfred Park towards the city of Sydney was appropriate for a man who had also served as an alderman on the City Council. James Jones, the 'overseer of the domains', was asked to furnish a plan for the garden, which, although larger than the usual terrace, conformed to the pattern of a long rectangular block. The solution proposed delighted the flamboyant O'Connor. The garden was laid out in beds and walks in the form of his own initials, 'DOC', and the beds were edged with tiles in a 'rope and rose' pattern manufactured by Crane & Sons. A wire-netting trellis for climbing roses was added in 1889. The planting undertaken by a gardener with the appropriate name of William Flowers indicates the appeal of roses and wisteria and the increasing popularity of palms: 'One palm for centre bed D. Bedding plants for three beds 8 x 6 ft [approx 2.5 x 2 m]; 18 dwarf roses for rose beds, 2 white roses, 3 dark clo. [colours], 12 dwarf shrubs, 1 wisteria & 2 other climbers'. Other plants found in the remnant gardens of terrace houses are most commonly the shade-tolerant *Aspidistra elatior* or 'cast-iron plant', a tough perennial with glossy dark foliage, and *Camellia japonica*. The latter is often seen as the principal planting for front gardens of Sydney terraces.

**ABOVE:** Ornamental-foliaged plants became increasingly popular from the mid-1860s and were sought-after specimens for the verandah or glasshouse. A brilliant example is *Cordyline fruticosa* var. '*Stricta*' (named as *Dracaena terminalis* in this 1870 illustration).

**ABOVE:** During the Boom period decorative urns were often placed on the pillars at the end of external stairs. This recently painted pottery urn originally had a salt-glaze finish, matching the salt-glazed decorative edging tiles which were featured in the garden.

**TOP RIGHT:** The richly modelled front of this Boom-style terrace in Old South Head Road, Bondi Junction, Sydney, is lost in its current monochrome colour scheme. Originally, a range of earthen colours with details picked out in contrasting colours or deeper pigments of the same hue would have made the detail clearly visible, even at a considerable distance.

**RIGHT:** Regional variations abound in Boom-style terrace house details. Decorative cast iron was used throughout Australia for verandah posts, brackets, valances and balustrades. The combination of timber and cast iron, uncommon in Melbourne and Sydney, was often used in Tasmanian terraces. Here a detail of the first-floor balcony balustrade and decorative brackets and frieze panels of a terrace house in St John Street, Launceston, shows a more conservative Boom-style composition that was often found in the more remote towns and cities.

# Federation

### MODEST OPTIMISM

### (1890–1920)

PREVIOUS PAGES: Each house in this Federation terrace at 50–56 Lower Fort Street, Millers Point, Sydney, is set back from its neighbour, maximising to striking effect the picturesque character of the gable ends. The powerful visual presence of the stepped, serried row of gables with a profile as sharp as a cross-cut saw, seen here in brilliant contrast against a clear blue sky, has been skilfully exploited by the designer. The false half-timbering of the upper reaches of each gable is here pulled out from the masonry to give the appearance of a pierced screen, a delightfully Australian deviation from the medievalism of the English Queen Anne Revival. The gardens are large enough for small trees. Fat branches of a frangipani dominate the house to the right. This small tree, eminently suited to small gardens in frost-free areas, increased in popularity and availability after the turn of the century.

In the last years of the nineteenth-century, Sir Henry Parkes, a champion of the federation of the six Australian colonies, expressed the hope, confidence and optimism of a young society looking to new ideas and social structures. Parallel to such high-minded ideals was a growing concern for social reform and improvements to public health, housing and education. Confidence in the future was tempered by an examination of past failures. By the end of the century the terrace house was beginning to be seen as an impediment to social progress and its central role as the norm for housing low- and middle-income families was on the wane. Surveying the social ills of the cities, some civic leaders saw the terrace house as a major cause of urban, even moral, decay. Such changes in attitudes, evident first as a social perception but later taking the form of political intervention, soon dealt a fatal blow to the terrace house in Australia. By the end of World War I it was essentially extinct, a victim of changes in building regulations as well as patterns of living, working and transport.

By the first decade of the twentieth century much of the terrace housing of inner-city areas had degenerated into squalid, disease-ridden slums. These unsanitary conditions, created by overcrowding, inadequate provision of clean water, drainage and sewerage, and poor access to natural light and ventilation, led to serious outbreaks of contagious and sometimes fatal diseases. Such conditions were at their worst in The Rocks in Sydney where bubonic plague, spread from infected rats

**TOP:** The use of decorative cast iron on verandahs and balconies did not entirely disappear in the Federation styles of terraces. 'Boro', which sits in a splendid row at 433–445 Glebe Point Road, Sydney, displays a certain conservatism in embracing Federation timbering. The habit of naming houses individually rather than the row, was a distinct trait of this period.

**ABOVE:** Although cast-iron balconies lingered, the general preference of Federation builders was decorative timberwork. The Art Nouveau style was never popular beyond the superficial use of motifs. Occasionally, however, an adventurous architect, such as Robert Haddon, used established materials to great effect. At Eastbourne House in Melbourne, built in 1906, he produced astonishing results with wrought instead of cast iron. Here, the sinuous Art Nouveau lines of a stylised peacock tail support the balustrade.

**ABOVE:** The boldness of the Federation terrace houses at 235–241 Beaufort Street, West Perth was never matched in the eastern states. Stout, square, painted timber verandah posts support a deeply arcaded timber screen above.

**LEFT:** The most exuberant Federation terraces showed a decided preference for an open gable facing the street. Numbers 433–445 Glebe Point Road, Sydney, boast an eclectic mixture of elements: pencil sharp finials, fretted barge boards and an abstracted hint of English medieval half-timbering.

**Above:** Eastbourne House, Melbourne, is something of an architectural cocktail. Its eclectic influences include principles of the English Arts and Crafts movement (honesty in the use of materials), Continental Art Nouveau (fluid wrought ironwork) mixed with a liberal dash of English Queen Anne Revival (face red brickwork) and Gothic Revival garnishes (wall ribbing). The recipe could well have been disastrous. In Robert Haddon's deft design, however, it worked well, producing a great Federation achievement.

**Left:** Never was unpainted cement render used with such delicate and lyrical beauty as in Haddon's stylised Art Nouveau floral motifs on the parapet entablature of Eastbourne House.

RIGHT: A pair of semi-detached houses in Stanmore Road, Enmore, Sydney, a house type popular in the Federation period, are little more than Boom-style houses with a new set of clothes. Solid respectability rather than flair or flamboyance was intended and clearly achieved in the design of these houses. The front gardens of this period were often kept as neatly trimmed lawn with no other embellishment.

ABOVE: The design of the verandah post capitals in Haddon's Eastbourne House displays a light-hearted wit rarely seen in the great mass of Federation terrace houses. Sadly, few similar flights of fancy will be discovered elsewhere in Australia by the Federation enthusiast.

escaping from ships, broke out in 1900. Evidence of urban decay was also widespread in other areas of inner-city terrace housing such as Surry Hills in Sydney and Carlton in Melbourne.

## FEDERATION FEATURES

The Federation terrace house derives its stylistic characteristics from the prevalent housing type of its period, the modest freestanding Federation cottage or bungalow. While the term Federation is used to denote both a period and a clearly identifiable architectural style, its use as a descriptive stylistic tag has divided architectural historians in Australia. Sydney-based writers tend to use it either to describe a style or to mark a period. Elsewhere in Australia the term is not so widely used. In Melbourne the terms Edwardian or Queen Anne Revival are often preferred.

The typical Federation house can be readily identified by its use of unpainted and unrendered red brickwork, and a complex roof made up of projecting gables and hips clad with unglazed terracotta Marseilles pattern tiles. Standing out from the roofs in picturesque profile stand towers, turrets, chimneys, finials and ridge cresting, while from the walls protrude square, circular

LEFT: The Federation semi-detached houses at 61–63 Stanmore Road in Enmore, Sydney, represent a significant variation to the genre. Although the design of this pair owes a strong stylistic debt to the Boom-style Italianate, the use of unpainted face brickwork and the quirky sash windows with small panes at top and bottom indicate a desire to produce effects of prettiness and quaintness. During the Federation period, wood was used extensively for decorative fretwork and fences. Wooden gates were usually a combination of bevelled posts, turned spindles, and tongue-and-groove panelling set in picket fences. Cast-iron palisade fences were also used.

**ABOVE:** Liberties taken by designers with windows are among the many charms of the Federation house. Although the tripartite double-hung sash window has its origins in Australian architecture of Regency times, Federation designers used considerable imagination in adapting building materials to new stylistic ends. The parlour window of 63 Lower Fort Street, Millers Point, Sydney, displays side sashes which would have challenged the window joiner's art.

**ABOVE:** It is unusual to see a single full-blooded Federation terrace inserted into an otherwise Victorian-era terrace streetscape. In Thomson Street, Darlinghurst, is one of Sydney's most delightful terraces, built around 1905, on the subdivision of the Riley Estate.

**RIGHT:** Picturesque-style modulation of the street facade of terraces did not allow designers the degree of freedom possible with the freestanding Federation house. 152–156 Melville Street, West Hobart, exploits to the greatest possible extent the Federation trait of breaking the main façade into a series of geometrically rich and visually complex planes and surfaces. The verandah bows out to accommodate a bay window which rises from the parlour on the ground floor through to the main bedroom above, and ending in a shallow peaked roof.

**LEFT:** The spoils of rich mining ventures and a desire to outdo the eastern states are visible on the houses of Perth. The terraces at 225–227 Beaufort Street, West Perth, are unmatched in their generosity of scale. The roofscape with its upstanding pediment gable ends and entablature above the party wall, and the vigour and scale of the turned and fretted timberwork of the verandah and balconies, remind us how few Federation terraces realised their full potential.

and octagonal window bays. Verandah posts, brackets and frieze panels, typically made of cast iron in Victorian terraces, were now made of carved, fretted or turned timber. Although the restrictive plan of the terrace house did not allow such a free reign, the Federation terrace can be recognised by its use of Marseilles roof tiles, tuck-pointed face brickwork and decorative timber verandah posts and brackets.

## MATERIAL INNOVATIONS

The Federation terrace was generally more sound than its predecessors. The Victorian fashion for plastering over the external walls provided little incentive to the bricklayer to develop and extend the art. In contrast, the Federation taste for unrendered or face brickwork prompted important developments in building practices. Because of the escalating cost of labour, it was technological developments in the manufacture of building materials rather than improvements in craftsmanship that began to dominate building practices.

Among the new concerns were increased durability of materials combined with improved ease of construction. Bricks—reds for the front façade, commons for the back—were fired at higher temperatures and therefore were harder and more durable, if less visually appealing. These advances were not matched in their laying, at least in the Federation terrace house. Otherwise rough joints were given the appearance of extraordinary precision with a little sleight of hand—or trowel. Tuck pointing, originally a Georgian device used for finely gauged brickwork over windows and doors, was applied to entire façades. It consisted of traditional lime mortar joints set flush to the surface of the brick and coloured to match it. Thin lines of fine, white, lime putty, each about five millimetres wide, were laid with precision over the real, hidden joint of the brick and trimmed with a straight edge and knife. As ever, the show and decoration was always at the front of the house; tuck pointing of good quality red bricks was rarely if ever used at the back. Of greater importance was the other

great innovation in brickwork, the double-skin external brick wall with an internal cavity. Variously claimed as an Australian, American or British invention, it was a major advance in preventing the penetration of damp.

Internally, the influence of the English Arts and Crafts Movement was often apparent in the decorative detail of the joinery and, occasionally, in the plasterwork as well. In Victorian or Boom-style terrace houses the typical chimneypiece was of either white or coloured marble, or of timber painted to simulate it. The Federation chimneypiece, however, was a more fanciful concoction of carved or fretted timberwork with flying brackets and intermediate shelves. In more elaborate houses an overmantel consisting of delicately bracketed shelving and mirrored back panels provided the householder with

LEFT: Whatever the extent of fashionable detailing in the public areas of the Federation house the strictly utilitarian back rooms changed little. In the kitchen of this 1905 terrace in Sydney's Glebe only the glazed white ceramic tiles around the 'fireplace' betray its period. The use of the tiles became practical with the advent of the gas stove, allowing the fastidious cook to keep the kitchen clean of ash and smoke.

BELOW: The interiors of most Federation terraces display a high degree of stylistic conservatism. Often the decorative scheme of the typical Federation house relies to a great degree on the established Boom-style taste, as shown here. The only significant departure was perhaps in the ceiling plasterwork where factory-made pre-cast fibrous gypsum plaster panels quickly replaced lime plastered cornices and ceiling flats.

LEFT: The exuberance of detailing of the Federation terrace was usually greater inside the house. Here the impact of the Aesthetic Movement's love of 'Art for Art's sake' is clear in the elaborate overmantel of a house in Glebe, Sydney. Mirrors (to reflect the rich patterns and colours of the William Morris wallpaper) and a multitude of niches and shelves (to display pottery, art glass and repoussé copperware) indulged the keen collector of artistic artefacts.

ample nooks and crannies for displaying collections of pottery, hand-beaten copperware or other aesthetic objects. The timber was usually stained a rich mahogany colour, varnished or shellacked.

## THE USE OF ART NOUVEAU

The gradual increase in the use of industrially manufactured building materials, appliances and fittings left their mark on the Federation terrace. Cast-fibrous plaster decorative ceiling panels and cornices, which were factory made, revolutionised the plastering trade, bringing to an end the use of lath-and-plaster ceilings and cornices, both of which had previously been applied in situ. Popular patterns of the time included stylised plants and flowers in the flowing, sinuous lines of the Art Nouveau style from Europe. Australian native animal and flower designs were used occasionally in large Federation houses but rarely in terraces. Stained glass, usually in fanlights and sidelights around the front door, often featured abstract plant forms with a distinct Art Nouveau flavour.

The crusades of the social reformers contributed to major advances in health and hygiene standards of house design. Technological innovations included electric lighting and significant improvements to the plumbing and fittings of kitchens and bathrooms. Gas hot-water heaters were installed above the bathtub and the shower made its appearance; the lavatory moved inside the house, into or beside the bathroom; and in rarer cases, reticulated hot and cold water was introduced. In the kitchen gas cookers replaced wood-fired fuel stoves.

## NEATLY FENCED LAWNS

Changing fashion did little to affect the way in which gardens were laid out, although their appearance was subtly altered by the gradual introduction of different plants and fence styles. With the aspirations of the general public increasingly turning to the ideal of the detached house in a garden suburb, the semi-detached house rather than the terrace became a more popular form of attached housing.

One appropriate foil for the Federation house was a large expanse of buffalo grass lawn. Curiously, this model had an impact on the front gardens of the terrace houses of this period. Often, where the terrace house was on a higher ground level than the street and space was limited, the solution was to plant the entire garden with buffalo or couch. It was then left devoid of any other embellishment. The challenge for the gardener of the household must have been to keep this lawn neat and well-trimmed.

ABOVE: This detail from the parapet of Eastbourne House in Melbourne is one of a few examples where the Art Nouveau style adorned terrace houses. When Art Nouveau did make an appearance, it was usually in this thin, two-dimensional form.

RIGHT: 63 Lower Fort Street, Millers Point, Sydney, is a Federation period terrace stylistically caught between new and old architectural fashions. The use of cast iron on the balustrade, the wrought iron palisade fence and polychrome brickwork were hangovers from Victorian taste, whilst the picturesque-style expression of the open gable end and its timberwork heralded the arrival of English Queen Anne Revival.

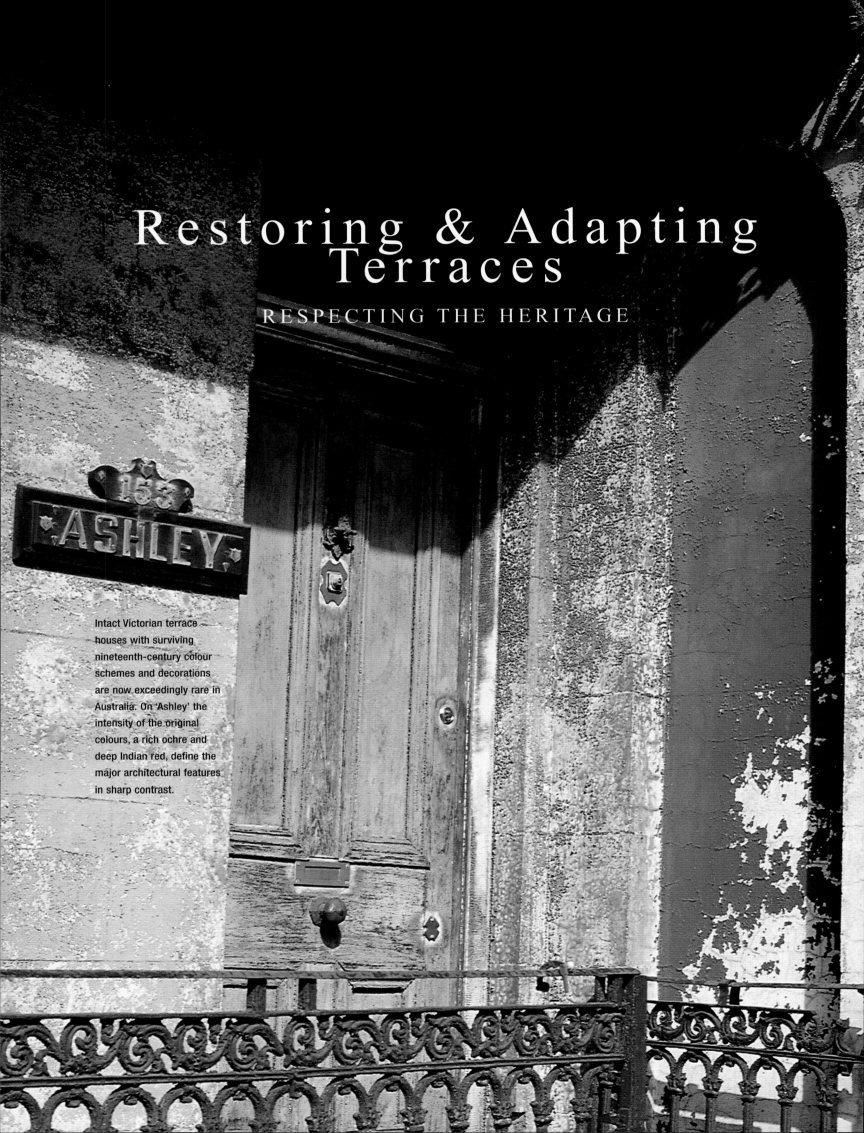

# Restoring & Adapting Terraces

## RESPECTING THE HERITAGE

Intact Victorian terrace houses with surviving nineteenth-century colour schemes and decorations are now exceedingly rare in Australia. On 'Ashley' the intensity of the original colours, a rich ochre and deep Indian red, define the major architectural features in sharp contrast.

'Ashley' is located only two kilometres from Sydney's city centre but has not been lived in for a generation. Despite the decrepit appearance of the building and the neighbouring terrace, very little work needs to be done to the exterior fabric except for repairs to the front door. While most rennovators would want the final look of a house to be less derelict in appearance, these terraces have a history. A new owner should savour and conserve the wonderful patina of age without making the house look like a skilful reconstruction.

The terrace house lost popularity soon after World War I, and until the 1960s the detached house in the suburbs was overwhelmingly favoured by Australians as their preferred type of housing. A growth in public transport systems assisted their move to the suburbs and for the first time trams, railways, buses and ferries allowed city-dwellers to live a considerable distance from their work. The shift to outlying suburbs was accelerated after World War II by the increasing affordability of private cars. But despite the advantages that the double-fronted, freestanding bungalow offered—large gardens, easy accommodation for cars, and room for extensions—the physical distance from the city centre and its attractions, lack of local amenities, and the need for long-distance commuting eventually encouraged many to rediscover the sense of urbanity that the more densely populated nineteenth-century city had to offer.

### RENOVATED OR ORIGINAL?

The first question facing the intending terrace-house buyer is whether to look for a fully renovated house or one substantially intact but in need of major care and attention. Each has its advantages and its responsibilities. The preferred option for many is to acquire an original, unrenovated, intact terrace. Sadly, the stock of traditional terrace houses throughout Australia, despite the protection that most enjoy, is gradually dwindling due to permitted and some illegal demolition and each year the task of finding such a property has become more difficult, and generally more

Respect for the patina of age should stop short of retaining any earlier vandalism of inappropriate, cheap and destructive 'improvements'. The insertion of three casement windows in this house demonstrates a crude way of increasing daylight into the house.

expensive. Houses that have been lived in by the same family for one or more generations and deceased estates offer the best chance. Although the astute terrace detective will scour the real estate pages for the sale of a house from a deceased estate, he or she will not be alone in this quest.

The main reason for intact terrace houses surviving unaltered is the previous owners' lack of money for repairs or improvement, but even intact terrace houses are likely to have suffered poor or little maintenance and the prospective buyer needs to carefully assess the physical condition of the house before purchase. Any intending buyer should first check the extent of physical damage to the building fabric. While many unsightly defects may be apparent, it is critical to distinguish between superficial damage and more serious faults. The most important defects involve structural instability, water penetration in all its forms, and biological attack, whether fungal or by insects.

## STRUCTURAL PROBLEMS

Cracking in wall plaster, the most common evidence of structural damage to the masonry walls, will usually have occurred due to uneven settlement or movement of the foundations. In some cases settlement may have occurred soon after the house was built and the structure left in a state of equilibrium, preventing further movement. The correct diagnosis of structural weakness or failure is not a matter for the amateur, and wherever it is suspected, an expert opinion should be sought from a structural engineer or another suitably qualified professional in the structural trade.

Water damage of some sort is likely to be found in most old terrace houses. Virtually no building material escapes completely unscathed from the continued presence of damp. There are three types of damp, each classified according to its source. The first, and perhaps the most common form, is rising damp where moisture rises up through capillary action from the foundations

**ABOVE:** New dormer windows and environmentally responsible alterations, such as water tanks and solar collectors, can be integrated with the traditional terrace. The regeneration of a row in Mary Anne Street, Ultimo, Sydney shows eloquent results.

**BELOW:** As the chimney is a critical element in the composition of a terrace, it should be demolished only in extreme cases of structural danger. Regular maintenance of chimneys, roofs, gutters and roof flashings will prevent heavy repair costs.

and footings. Nineteenth-century terraces either lacked damp-proof courses altogether or used techniques, such as a continuous layer of roofing slates, which subsequently failed. The second type, penetration damp, occurs where water seeps through walls laterally. Heavy rain, leaking gutters and downpipes, water pipes coming into contact with open joints in brickwork, or porous bricks and render are the most common causes of penetration damp. The third type, descending damp, signals failures in roofs, gutters and downpipes. Another broad field of building fabric decay or damage is that caused by fungal attack such as wet or dry rot. This is usually associated with damage caused by the various forms of water penetration.

## HOW DO YOU CHOOSE AN ARCHITECT?

Before undertaking substantial alterations to a terrace— whether intact or highly altered—the renovator must

**RIGHT:** Roof ladders can aid inspections and repairs. The chimney pot, usually made of salt-glazed terracotta or earthenware in Victorian times or unglazed terracotta in the Federation era, is critical to the chimney's appearance. It also increases flue draught and reduces rainwater leaks. Damaged, old chimney pots can be replaced with sound recycled pots or appropriate modern reproductions.

decide whether to use the services of an appropriately skilled architect. Where the intended changes are more than cosmetic, and especially where substantial structural change and demolition is involved, investing in the services of a well-chosen architect will always repay the financial commitment involved. Choosing an architect is not an easy task, especially for those who have not used one before. Relying on reputation alone is not enough and the prudent renovator should first do a little homework to ensure an appropriate and successful choice is made for both architect and client. A shortlist of possible prospective architects should be compiled from diverse sources: word-of-mouth, published articles on particular projects, or completed works known to the prospective client. Where a conservation specialist is needed, the local chapter of the Royal Australian Institute of Architects (RAIA) or the appropriate government planning authority in each state will usually be able to provide a list of recognised expert practitioners.

The wise client should select an architect with a proven record of working on small-scale building works and one who has a good understanding of traditional detailing, even if much of the planned alteration work is in a modern idiom. For some, the choice will be assisted by obtaining a list of recent architectural award winners, available from the local chapters of the RAIA. There are, however, a great many excellent architects who do not enter their work for the annual awards and who should not be overlooked on this account. Having made a shortlist of perhaps two or three, make an appointment to meet the architects and discuss your needs. At the meeting you will most likely see examples of their completed work and it is preferable if you can speak to the clients for these projects in order to help you form your own judgment before commissioning an architect to work on your behalf.

**ABOVE:** A verandah appears to have been removed from this terrace and the repair is less than satisfactory. Traditional brick mortar used little or no cement. Today, cement is added because of ease of use, cheapness, availability and strength. Cement render is less porous than lime-based renders or stuccoes and may cause or exacerbate damp problems, as has happened here. There is also a danger of the brickwork cracking with any wall movement.

**ABOVE:** Much of the subtlety and visual texture of the Victorian terrace house roof will be lost if the break in line and plane of the main and balcony roofs are combined when re-roofing takes place. The house on the right retains its separate bull-nosed balcony roof whereas its neighbour has lost its, along with much of the character of its roof line.

**RIGHT:** The popularity of applying sprayed concrete finishes to terrace house exteriors has waned but should be banned outright. The evident claims of the applier have not been fulfilled as this sad example shows: the better part has fallen off, leaving behind unsightly scars.

It is particularly important that an appropriate philosophical approach to the treatment of the old house is worked out before the house's new functional needs study and architectural brief are considered. A proper understanding of, and respect for, the original building fabric to guide the hand and the heart is essential for a really successful result. In many places where terraces stand in Conservation Areas designated by the local council, statutory planning controls require professional assessment of the impact that any proposed works will have on the old fabric of the house. In these circumstances an architect or heritage consultant specialising in architectural conservation is needed. The nationally accepted principles of conservation practice in Australia are set out in the *Burra Charter for the Conservation of Places of Cultural Significance*, commonly referred to as the 'Burra Charter'. General readers and professionals alike are also strongly advised to consult Meredith Walker and Peter Marquis-Kyle's easy-to-understand *Illustrated Burra Charter*, which is available from National Trust bookshops or from any good bookshop. Full publication details of these books are set out in the bibliography.

The most important principle contained in the Burra Charter is that the fabric of a building deserves not only to be respected but a thorough understanding and assessment of it established before any decisions are made which will lead to its removal or any other irreversible change. The process of analysis and interpretation leads to the determination of a 'statement of cultural significance'. Put more simply, this means 'why and how your terrace house is important'. The statement is then used as a basis for informing and guiding appropriate approaches to the care of the old elements of the fabric as well as to planning the new. Working out an appropriate approach to planning your renovations can also be greatly assisted by referring to James Semple Kerr's *The Conservation Plan*. Although intended for professional conservation practitioners, the book sets out clearly the steps local councils in Australia require when owners submit development applications for alterations to buildings of heritage significance.

**TOP LEFT:** Traditional nineteenth-century roofing materials were timber shingles, slate, and corrugated iron sheeting. The exception was the Federation era when unglazed terracotta Marseilles pattern tiles were used. Pressed-metal roof-cladding imitating terracotta tiles is not a traditional terrace restoration material.

**ABOVE LEFT:** Every old building tells a story which archeological evidence can decode. The removal of upper balconies often leaves traces of the old fabric. In this case the stepped lead flashing records the line of the original balcony roof.

**ABOVE RIGHT:** The main traditional roofing material of Victorian terraces was slate; however, to replace old roofs with slate today can cost three times that of corrugated steel. This house has been successfully re-roofed in corrugated steel. However, during the 1960s and 1970s there was the misguided practice of removing original render to expose the brickwork, which was never intended to be seen. The exposed bricks were often carelessly laid, unattractive and very susceptible to decay and water penetration.

**LEFT:** The rough texture of cement render is loved by some builders but, as this example shows, it should be avoided as it can permanently disfigure exterior walls.

The enclosing of verandahs and balconies must be handled sensitively. Light construction, which is reversible, should be used, and the new windows should follow the general size and proportion of the existing façade. The crude masonry used in this example will make it difficult to restore the terrace to its former glory.

## SCALE OF WORKS AND BUDGETS

If you are planning large-scale renovations you will need to assess, realistically and logistically, the advantages and drawbacks of staying put while the builder works around you. Staying in the house during building work has the apparent advantage of saving the cost of renting temporary accommodation. However, coping with noise, disruption and mess takes a heavy toll on even the most stoic renovator. Great strains are placed on the personal relationships of stay-put rennovators, whose numbers swell the offices of divorce lawyers and crisis counsellors each year. It is also worth remembering that most builders will charge clients more if they remain resident on the site. Many will cope without a kitchen but the lack of a bathroom makes any house almost uninhabitable. Where small children are involved the wise choice is simply to move out.

Renovated houses may have the advantage of being immediately livable but more often than not the major focus of earlier alterations will have been the kitchen and bathroom. Here personal tastes are so variable it is rare indeed for a new buyer to be completely satisfied with earlier improvements. Patience and depth of pocket should always be the main guides for those contemplating major alterations.

## EXTERNAL ELEMENTS

The keen terrace-house restorer should start by making an inventory of all of the essential external functional and decorative elements of the house. Inevitably some items will have been removed or altered.

Perhaps the largest single building element which people are tempted to demolish is the chimney. All chimneys, whether seen from the street or from the back lane, are important parts of the architectural composition of the house and make a significant contribution to the streetscape. Generally, they should not be removed. If the householder wishes to re-use the fireplaces the flues can be cleaned relatively cheaply by an experienced chimney sweep. No longer are Dickensian methods used: modern

**RIGHT:** With imagination and sensitivity the goal of increased space without compromising the façade can be achieved, as this balcony enclosure of a Sydney terrace demonstrates.

**TOP:** The enclosure of the balcony on the right may appear crude but the original cast-iron balustrade could be underneath the material. To restore a balcony, determine if the old iron survives and employ someone with the skills to reinstate the cast iron, whether old or new.

**ABOVE:** The back of a terrace can offer great scope for increasing interior space. By lifting the main roof behind the ridge from boundary to boundary and to the back wall, an attic room can be added. The design of this addition in Sydney's Darlinghurst demonstrates good architectural planning and excellent conservation practice.

industrial vacuum cleaners efficiently, if unromantically, remove a century's accumulated soot and dust. Although most leaking chimneys can be easily repaired, a correct diagnosis is required first. Water may penetrate a chimney due to a lost or ineffective chimney pot, missing or cracked mortar in the brickwork, cracking in the chimney rendering or stucco, or lost or broken flashings. Just as the chimney is an integral part of the silhouette of the typical terrace house, its chimney pots are like the icing on the cake. Sound old chimney pots should be left in place wherever possible. Where some or all of the original pots have been lost it is often possible to buy replacements to match. Cowls made up of tapering slates are easily replaced or repaired but the skilled hands of a good slater will be necessary.

One dilemma faced by many terrace-house owners is the difficult decision of what to do with an original slate roof which is past its useful life. Depending on the location, the extent of air-borne pollution and exposure to corrosive elements such as the ocean, a well-laid slate

These attic dormer windows are in an advanced state of decay. The window on the left originally had a double-hung sash and the present installation of adjustable louvres is not in keeping with the traditional design. To restore properly, the detail will need to be copied from its adjacent mate before it, too, falls into total disrepair and the design is lost forever.

roof should last up to 120 years, or even longer. An expert opinion from a reputable slater is necessary to assess the state of the roof. Sometimes selective patching may be practical but where the only realistic option is total replacement, a difficult decision must be made. A good slate roof costs between twice and three times the price of corrugated steel.

If your budget does not allow for full replacement in slate the only acceptable alternative is corrugated steel. Avoid the use of ribbed-steel roof decking, pressed metal sheeting simulating tiles, artificial slates (whether fibrous-cement or concrete), terracotta, or concrete roof tiles. Only where a Federation-style terrace house was originally clad in unglazed terracotta Marseilles tiles should they be replaced in the same material. Corrugated steel, more widely but no longer accurately known as galvanised or 'gal' iron, was a very common roofing material from the middle of the nineteenth century

onwards. In Victorian and Federation times it was quite usual for the main roof to be slate, with corrugated iron sheeting used for the kitchen and laundry wing. Corrugated steel sheeting with a protective coating of a zinc-aluminium alloy, produced commercially under the name Zincalume, is now used widely in preference to galvanised corrugated steel sheeting. However, care must be taken to use zinc, not lead, flashings; the latter would eventually lead to corrosion due to a chemical reaction between the two metals.

## REPLACING IRON LACE AND STUCCO

Enclosing a first-floor front verandah is one of the most common alterations made to Australian terrace houses. While this had the advantage of gaining a little extra internal space, it was at the expense of the external appearance of the terrace. Fortunately, this alteration is easily reversed. With any luck the original decorative

The corner grocery shop, like all shops, is subject to greater passing fashions than most buildings. Of all the details lost from Victorian terraces few are as severe as the loss of the first-floor balcony. It is likely from the surviving evidence on this shop with a residence above that a timber cantilevered balcony swept around the major street frontages. Inappropriate alterations have also occurred: timber sashes have been changed to aluminium and a proportion of the ground floor window near the front door has been enlarged.

cast iron may survive intact under the enclosure. Where it has been damaged or removed, old cast iron can often be found to replace it. If new cast iron is required an appropriate pattern must be chosen. This can be done by looking at nearby houses. If your terrace is one of a row it is highly likely that all the houses in that row shared the same pattern. Most capital cities have dealers who sell recycled architectural detailing and other items and they may stock old cast-iron lace or be willing to find it for you. If this fails you can either choose another pattern or, with the assistance of a cooperative neighbour, borrow a panel of the desired design and have it recast. This option can be costly but is extremely rewarding for the serious restorer.

Over time the loss of stucco, whether smooth, decorative, cast or moulded, often occurs to many Victorian and Boom-style terraces. In the latter case the losses tend to be greatest on those parts of the building most exposed to the elements—parapets, urns, balustrades and other decorative features. Here there is no substitute for skill and expertise. To achieve satisfactory results you should engage only craftsmen who can demonstrate that they can undertake repairs and reconstruction skilfully. Be alert to the builder whose universal panacea for all masonry ills is a liberal coating of cement-rich render.

### BALCONIES

The architectural detective may be richly rewarded by a careful examination of a building's fabric, as previous owners are likely to have subtracted from as well as added to the building over time. First-floor balconies, especially those that were cantilevered, have often been casualties of wear and tear—or the heavy hand of the improver. Reconstruction of a lost balcony can be

difficult, particularly where there is no physical evidence in the building fabric itself or reliable documentary evidence such as photographs. Examining the surface of the house will often reveal some clues. The original line of a concave or convex verandah roof may survive in the stucco or in a line of remaining stepped lead flashings. The sawn-off remnants of projecting floor joists may await interpretation and help to solve the mystery. With the help of such clues and evidence from old photographs or from similar houses nearby, missing verandahs and other lost elements can be reconstructed with confidence.

### WINDOWS AND DOORS

By far the most disfiguring of all the inappropriate alterations that can be made to a terrace house is the removal of the original doors and windows along the front or other principal façade. While the front-door opening is seldom altered, the windows are a different matter. Regrettably, it was once common for 'improvers' to remove original double-hung timber sash windows and replace them with sliding aluminium windows, a practice that can only be considered an act of architectural barbarism, which is now rarely permitted these days by local councils. Fortunately, it is now possible to find skilled traditional joiners who can readily make up these window sashes. Where the windows are of the double-hung type, take great care to ensure that they are made in the traditional way using sash cords and weights. Joinery is expensive so be well advised to seek advice from a conservation architect to avoid costly mistakes.

**ABOVE:** The appropriate use of traditional colours will bring an old terrace to life. Decorative cast-iron balustrades were painted in deep, bold colours. This detail of a balustrade illustrates the striking presence that an Indian red colour produces.

ABOVE: The replacement of original roofs with inappropriate materials is still common. For ease and cost savings, the upstanding firewalls of these terraces in a common roof plane have been shaved off and modern, glazed Marseilles tiles replace slate or corrugated steel.

LEFT: Few people approach the restoration of a largely intact terrace house with the zeal for historical accuracy achieved by Clive Lucas Stapleton & Partners for the Sydney Cove Authority. The largely derelict service wings of Jobbins Terrace in Gloucester Street, The Rocks, was recreated with great attention to detail.

## A QUESTION OF COLOUR

No issue seems to divide terrace owners and experts alike more than the choice of colours. Traditional colour schemes (now often known by the unfortunate term 'heritage') have become widely accepted since the 1970s with the growing success of the conservation movement. Although the question of what constitutes an appropriate traditional colour scheme is too large a topic to canvass in detail in this book, some general principles are worthy of consideration. For detailed and erudite guidance on this subject Ian Stapleton's *Colour Schemes for Old Australian Houses* and *More Colour Schemes for Old Australian Houses* are strongly recommended.

Externally, the body of the masonry walls were traditionally painted earthen and stony colours: umbers, siennas, drabs, a rich array of browns from near buff to pumpkin, and even striking Indian reds. Raised and projecting stucco mouldings were painted most often in a related darker or lighter (but boldly contrasting) colour

RIGHT: The decorative plasterwork of terrace houses is among the finest and most beautiful of ornamental detail. In the original parlour of this 1881 terrace, an exquisitely complex lime-plaster cornice, run in-situ, has been carefully repaired and restored.

BOTTOM: Many rooms in Victorian terraces that were not intended to be seen by visitors were built without cornices. Where it is not possible to save old lath-and-plaster ceilings, replacements in new plasterboard can be set with a shadow detail that clearly indicates the material is not part of the original fabric yet respects its design intention.

to highlight the architectural detailing. Window shutters and sashes were often painted a dark, bronzy green with the window frames in a contrasting rich cream. Front doors were usually a bold, dark colour matching the shutter colour. Cast iron was commonly painted bronze green or dark Indian red. On Boom-style houses it was not uncommon to pick out decorative elements in lighter greens and creams. Eau de Nil, a dull green, was invariably used externally on the underside of the first-floor verandah boards and floor structure.

The choice of colours used internally is, if anything, even more fraught with difficulty than that of the exterior. Here the relationship between the householder and the colour scheme is more intimate and prolonged. Traditional painted colour schemes were often enriched with highly coloured decorative wallpapers and friezes. Cornices were usually picked out in several colours, often quite striking in contrast and hue. If a very general rule of thumb can be made, richness of colour and pattern were common, especially where the occupants had sufficient means for decoration. While authentic colour schemes will not please all contemporary owners of traditional houses, wherever possible it is important to leave the evidence of earlier decorative schemes for later generations of terrace-house fanciers. This is easily and cheaply achieved by merely painting over the old.

## INTERIORS: BALANCING OLD AND NEW

Internal alterations to a terrace house present the owner with a truly daunting range of options. Few original nineteenth-century terrace-house bathrooms and kitchens survive and those that do properly deserve to be preserved as house museums. For the great majority of terrace-house owners, living with the services of past generations is neither realistic nor reasonable. Where the house is relatively intact and unchanged, it is preferable

**ABOVE:** This fanlight in a Boom-style house in Summer Hill, Sydney, casts pools of splendid red-patterned light. The panes comprise layers of coloured glass laminated over clear glass and etched or carved to produce the highly decorative motifs.

**RIGHT:** The triumph of illusion can be complete in skilled hands. This detail of the grainer's art shows finely honed oak and walnut for the price of painted pine.

The owner of a house with its original decorative finishes intact is indeed lucky and privileged. In this magnificent 1890 Boom-style home, the work of the well-known Glebe and Summer Hill builder David Elphinstone, the graining of the doors linking the parlour and dining room has survived in excellent condition. The painter's skill has imitated walnut on the styles and oak graining in the fielded panels between.

**ABOVE:** The restoring of a very intact Boom-style terrace house with absolute faithfulness to the date of its construction can lead the unwary or the over-zealous into dangerous error. Here the surviving Congoleum tread covering, dating possibly from the 1920s and patterned like a Turkish carpet, has been kept as a vital element of the accumulated history of the house. If the householder finds the weight or pattern of history too heavy, he or she should carefully remove such important decorative finishes and store them safely on site to await a later resident.

**RIGHT:** Victorians had a deep love of lively colour and pattern. Sometimes great subtlety was used to add variety to any decorative element of the building fabric. Here each baluster, obscured by later painting, was made of a different wood, Australian red cedar on the left, pine on the right. If you acquire a house of such refinement keep the interior decorator at bay or on a short leash or, best of all, off the site entirely.

**FAR RIGHT:** The finest piece of joinery in almost all terrace houses is the staircase and in most cases it is the most complex. Repairs and restoration are best avoided by the enthusiastic owner whose zeal outstrips their skill. Poor work may be impossible or very expensive to undo. The staircase of this fine Boom-style house was once buried beneath layers of paint. The owner, under expert guidance, stripped it back to reveal its original character. Dados were commonly painted in heavily trafficked areas such as hallways and stairs. Invariably the dado was painted in a darker colour to hide scuff marks and accumulated dirt.

if those areas which need to be most radically changed can be concentrated in particular locations, such as the kitchen, bathroom and laundry. One school of thought favours building kitchens and bathrooms in the style of the original house. Indeed many building material supply companies specialise in reproduction fittings made for this purpose. A note of caution needs to be sounded here because this approach is often philosophically dubious and practically misguided. Household technology and personal living habits have changed so much in the past eight or more decades that the notion of creating a bathroom, laundry or kitchen, which meets current performance and convenience expectations, in the style of a Victorian or Federation terrace house is nothing more than absurd. It is also at odds with the approach that builders of the time would have taken. Until the relatively recent fashion for nostalgic recreations, existing buildings were generally altered in line with fashions and technological advances current at the time. How does the fake Victorian kitchen incorporate the twin-door refrigerator, the dishwasher or the freezer?

**LEFT:** Throughout the nineteenth century traditional run lime-plaster cornices were painted in rich colours. Here the strong sense of colour follows that of the original, but a more subdued result can be achieved with a gentler off-white cream and a dash of warming yellow.

**BELOW:** Traditionally the dining room was seen as the man's domain, the parlour or (with)drawing room the ladies' realm. A useful key in deciphering gender usage is the colour of the chimneypiece: black was considered correct for men and white for women.

**LEFT:** The recreation of Victorian or Federation interiors can be rewarding. Here the owner decided to create a library in the front room on the first floor, the original main bedroom. The simplicity of the square set ceiling in its original form has been wisely left unaltered with emphasis placed on a strong wall colour—rich terracotta—and suitable furniture and carpets.

**BELOW:** This highly coloured ceiling rosette is characteristic of the Boom-style era of the terrace.

How does the Federation laundry accommodate the front-loading washing machine and clothes dryer? The answer is simple: do not consider this misguided solution. The most sensible, honest and, in all probability, most successful approach is to express the new building elements in a sympathetic but contemporary way while taking the utmost care to conserve the original building fabric.

Good design, combined with a sensitivity to the old, is most likely to satisfy modern requirements in adapting the traditional terrace house to contemporary needs while respecting its historic integrity. A successful balance between old and new can often be struck by retaining original door and window openings. Where this is not possible, consider incorporating replacements in similar materials to a contemporary design.

Sometimes a totally modern idiom can be used where the designer's hand is guided by the twin goals of respect for the old and the design integrity of the new. The kitchen wing of terrace houses has often been subject to change over time as each generation attempted to incorporate new levels of domestic comfort. Some elements of the original kitchen may lend themselves to new uses. For example, a surviving flue from the kitchen fireplace may provide a suitable vent for the exhaust fan of a modern electric or gas cooktop.

Today's interiors reflect the contemporary idiom. In this compact terrace house in Darlinghurst, Sydney, unconnected small spaces have been transformed into a large unified whole. By throwing two small rooms into one and creating a third in a Zen-inspired garden, a large living and dining area flows from the front door to the back lane. Stone, star jasmine and vibrant colour add to this tiny garden.

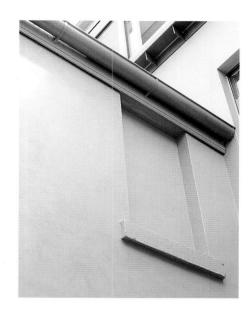

**ABOVE:** Working largely within the existing shell of a typical 1880s terrace house close to the centre of Darlinghurst's coffee shop strip, the architect has created fluid, open living spaces by removing old ceilings and wall partitions.

**TOP RIGHT:** Old windows no longer needed in the re-ordering of terrace houses can be readily made to disappear internally by the building of new partitions. Externally the window openings often form a critically important element of the composition of a façade, even on the rear service wing. In this example the original bathroom was extended into the adjacent bedroom of a typical 1880s terrace. Where the positioning of a new shower recess meant the original window was no longer required, the old opening was blocked up externally and left as part of the house's archaeology to tell its story of adaptation and change over time.

**RIGHT:** Even more radical intervention can lead to the creation of spatial arrangements unimaginable to the Victorian builder. Here the controlled and disciplined minimalism of architect Ian Moore has stripped away the old ceiling and internal walls to create a single new living, dining and sleeping space with an open mezzanine hovering above. Glass walls at the rear and skylights in the roof flood the space with light.

LEFT: This addition to an elaborate Boom-style terrace in Woollahra, Sydney, followed a sound design principle in positioning new rooms in a separate pavilion at the back, out of sight from the listed heritage streetscape in which it sits. Virginia Kerridge's design of the sitting/dining room/kitchen beneath the master bedroom is modern yet respectful in its relationship to the old fabric.

RIGHT: Virginia Kerridge placed a new entry between the new (out of sight to the right) and old sections of this terrace house in Woollahra. The garden, with a long water feature to one side, functions as an outdoor living room.

## DIGGING UP THE PAST

Few owners of terrace houses are fortunate enough to have remnants of the original garden layout. It is possible, however, that the original design is obscured by paving, concreting or changes in ground level design imposed at a later date. A gentle dig with a spade can sometimes reveal a path just below the ground level or evidence of garden edging tiles. Old photographs are an invaluable tool in gauging what the garden may have looked like. The local studies section of a municipal library or local historical society archives are good places to start any search for old photographs of both your own house and your area.

An appreciation of regional differences in the use of plants is important if the goal is to refashion an authentic garden. The use of the frangipani for terrace gardens in Melbourne, for example, would be an unusual choice but they are a common sight in Sydney, especially for early twentieth-century terraces. If there is no original front fence, choosing an appropriate style is important; publications by the National Trust in Victoria, the Department of Planning in New South Wales and other state government bodies can provide excellent guidance.

Of obvious interest in an area where space is at a premium is how the garden should function. For the occupants of many terrace houses the primary use for the backyard is providing an outside dining or entertaining area, combined with some area for storage and clothes drying. If the aim is to maintain the feel of a nineteenth- or early twentieth-century terrace, this can be achieved by the use of appropriate plants with a tree, such as a lemon, as the major planting and, perhaps, potted geraniums, ferns, glossy-leaved perennials and shrubs, such as viburnum and gardenia, as low-growing plants. Publications available on traditional and cottage gardening, such as those by Peter Cuffley and Trevor Nottle, provide lists of suitable plants for old gardens. The use of hard elements such as arbours, rose arches, lattice screens and wooden slatted shade houses in a style sympathetic to the period of the house also reinforces the image of an older garden. Sadly, there is an increasing tendency to demolish redundant outside lavatories which, along with the laneways the night cart used, are a reminder of how these houses worked. These structure can easily be transformed into wonderful storage spaces for garden tools and hardware or even an office.

**ABOVE:** A stone baluster, originally part of the pediment of the Chief Secretary's Building in Sydney, has been recycled as a garden ornament following essential repairs to the building. It supports a terracotta pot of bromeliads. Grown outdoors in frost-free environments, the stiff architectural and often colourful foliage of bromeliads lends variety to the confined garden.

**LEFT:** This greenhouse occupies the space formerly filled by an external staircase. At second-floor level, it provides a leafy retreat and screens a neighbouring rooftop from view.

**BELOW:** In a space no more than two metres wide, architect Alec Tzannes inserted a double-height steel-framed conservatory running parallel to the service wing of a Federation terrace. The traditional use of black and white checkerboard marble tiles was replicated at a more affordable cost in ceramic tiles.

**BELOW LEFT:** The shady front garden of a tiny terrace in the inner Sydney suburb of Rozelle is simply planted with a tree fern and ground cover. The necessary light and space for its successful growth was achieved by not replacing all the iron to the roof when the verandah was rebuilt.

**LEFT:** Clipped murrayas provide this garden in the Sydney suburb of Woollahra with form while not hiding the architecture of the house. Height in the garden comes from using a standard rose. Other plantings include grey santolina and hemerocallis (daylilies) which provide a splash of yellow.

**RIGHT:** This central circular bed in a garden at St Vincent Place, South Melbourne, is enclosed with a clipped hedge and surrounded by a brick path and flower beds.

**ABOVE:** Urns with trailing plants frame the decoratively painted window of this inner-Sydney terrace, 'Moe'. The shutters have curved heads to fit the window opening snugly. Underneath the window are the cast-iron spear-head finials of the palisade fence.

**RIGHT:** This garden, designed by the Sydney firm Mayne-Wilson and Associates, draws on nineteenth-century suggestions with its centrally placed urn on a plinth used as the focal point. The urn is planted with an agave. Brick paths are edged with mondo grass and seasonal colour in this semi-shaded garden is provided by perimeter plantings of camellias, clumps of azaleas and gardenias.

## KEEP IT SIMPLE

The front garden today still functions as it was originally intended—as an entrance area and ornamental setting for the house—in addition to the traditional role of demonstrating the taste of the occupants. The recommendation of nineteenth-century garden writers to keep the layout simple remains good advice. If the space is large enough, one of the many geometric pattern-book designs will provide the garden with an appropriate atmosphere. It is still possible to buy old edging tiles at auctions or demolition yards but a good alternative is to use reproduction terracotta edging tiles available from many nurseries. Brick edging is another option. This can be done in several ways: a saw-tooth pattern where the bricks are set at 45-degree angles; a plain upright vertical row; a head-to-tail row; or bricks set in a 'battlement' configuration with alternate vertical and horizontal bricks. Dwarf hedging provides a softer edge. The most popular choice in the past for this was box, but this is not always successful; an alternative, such as the mid-nineteenth century suggestion of thyme, may be a more suitable choice.

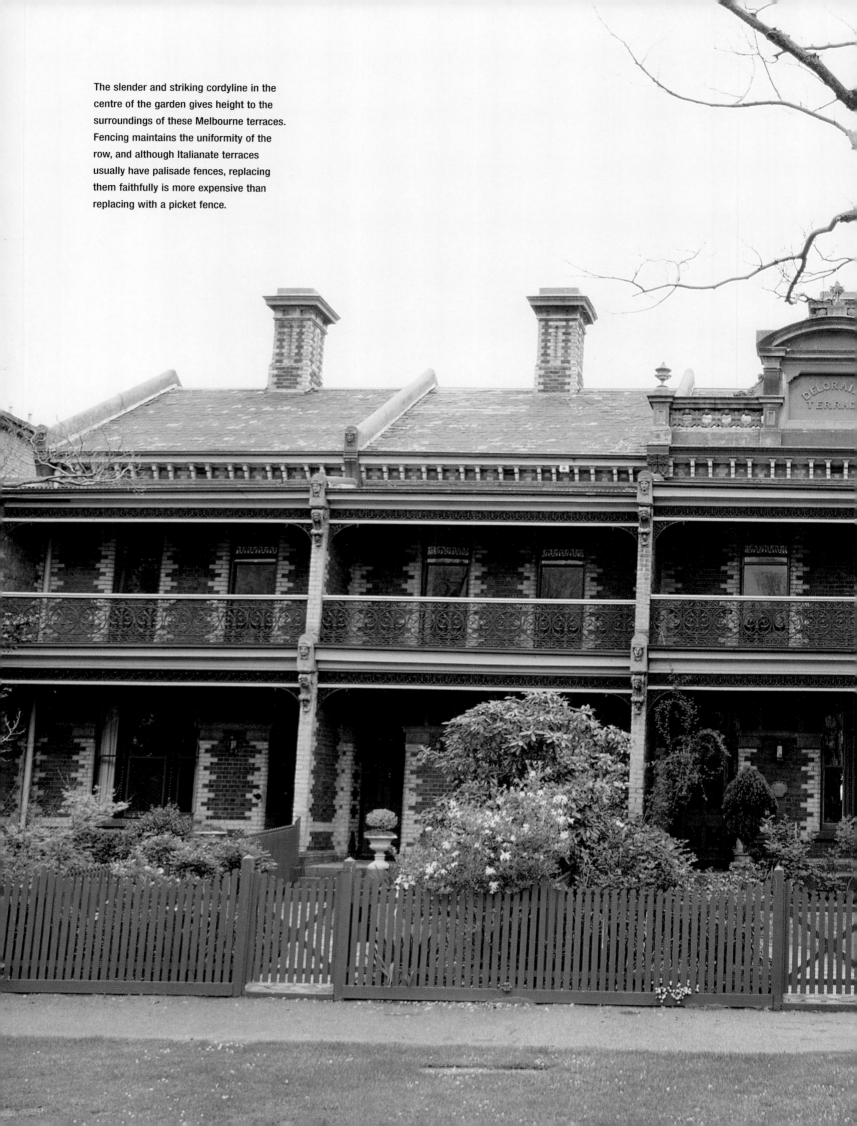

The slender and striking cordyline in the centre of the garden gives height to the surroundings of these Melbourne terraces. Fencing maintains the uniformity of the row, and although Italianate terraces usually have palisade fences, replacing them faithfully is more expensive than replacing with a picket fence.

In the 1970s the widespread enthusiasm for native gardens led to many small front gardens being planted with unsuitably sized trees such as eucalypts and casuarinas. Although this led to a welcome increase in the number of birds in the inner city, many terrace-house owners are now faced with blocked gutters, the expense of tree removal, and the prospect of structural damage. Small trees and shrubs are more appropriate choices for the front gardens of terrace houses. Height in a very small garden can be easily introduced by planting a tall, slim cordyline, one of the smaller palms, or a climbing rose on a vertical support.

If the desire is to keep the planting simple but more contemporary, succulents such as the architecturally impressive *agave attentuata* provide a low-maintenance but high-impact focus to a garden. These are especially impressive where the garden is above street level, allowing the curving arches of their enormous flower stems to be fully appreciated.

LEFT: This child's cubbyhouse now occupies the place where generations of chicken coops were found collapsed under garden refuse and privet in the backyard of this Federation terrace in Sydney. Nasturtiums, daisies and geraniums roam in the garden. A simple frame of bamboo and wire supports the climber Chilean jasmine or mandevilla.

BELOW: Artificial stone urns can be used effectively to provide a focus and height in a simple geometric layout.

ABOVE: A traditional design with terracotta-edged gravel path in an East Melbourne garden, a basic layout for owners wishing to reinstate a traditional terrace house garden.

BELOW: Concrete covers the original paths and partially obscures salt-glazed edging tiles in a garden with a remarkably intact layout in Glebe, Sydney. Mature camellias grow in symmetrically placed circular garden beds, further physical evidence of the original layout.

**ABOVE:** Various species of bamboo have been planted in Australian gardens since the early nineteenth century. This screen of hedged bamboo is used in the front garden of a terrace in the Sydney suburb of Paddington.

**RIGHT:** The Marguerite daisy, *Chrysanthemum frutescens* (now known as Paris daisy or *Argyrantemum*) has been a popular flower since colonial times and suits the terrace house garden.

**RIGHT:** The genus *Primula* has a large number of species of old-fashioned annuals and perennials suitable for small gardens. This example is commonly known as *polyanthus*.

**BELOW:** A variety of solutions for narrow front gardens in the Melbourne suburb of Fitzroy—parallel clipped hedges of staggered heights for one terrace and a uniform line of pots for another. The closing-in of verandahs detracts from the uniformity of terraced rows.

# Contemporary Designs

## A LIVING TRADITION

With a wider than average terrace site and a totally free hand, the skilful architect can rethink and adapt the traditional plan to accommodate contemporary living. The site of this new Paddington terrace house in Sydney, designed by Alec Tzannes, was never previously built upon. The architect allowed the house to be divided into two separate pavilions connected by an airy double-storeyed gallery. Between each a generous and totally private courtyard has access from the house on three sides.

The rediscovery of the traditional terrace house as a desirable form of housing in the 1960s began a boom in restoration and renovation that is still growing. While the traditional terrace house lent itself to modification and addition with varying degrees of success, many householders and architects recognised the need to reinterpret the terrace house to satisfy the lifestyles of the residents of the late twentieth century.

The contemporary terrace house falls into two distinct types. The first is the single residence, built as an 'infill' between existing terraces. These invariably fall within Conservation Areas, designated precincts of protected historic buildings, and restrictions apply to the design of new structures as well as alteration of old buildings. Successful results have depended to a large degree on the tenacity and patience of the client combined with the skill of the architect. To produce works of high-quality contemporary architecture while navigating the heritage and other planning controls of the local council is a process fraught with many difficulties.

Disagreements (even collisions) between council, designer and client are all too common. One of the most contentious areas of design concerns the relationship between the street facade of a contemporary terrace house and that of its Victorian or Federation neighbours. The challenge is to create a building in keeping with the area without recourse to poor copies of past styles.

The second type, now usually referred to as 'town houses' in the real estate trade, comprises terrace houses built in areas previously occupied by low-density housing beyond the immediate inner-city terrace belt or on former industrial sites. In either case the designer is not usually constrained by the limitations of nineteenth-century terrace house builders, such as land subdivisions, and, therefore, greater flexibility of the design of new terraces is possible.

**ABOVE:** A good architect can integrate the new into the old without a loss of integrity to either. This wide new terrace, designed by Alec Tzannes, uses traditional materials, such as coloured stucco and painted joinery, to relate the façade to an established Victorian streetscape.

**LEFT:** Fitting the contemporary terrace seamlessly into a streetscape of recognised heritage value is a challenge that few architects succeed in achieving. Here careful attention to the roof lines of the immediate neighbouring houses guides the composition of the street facade.

**ABOVE:** The design of this house by Alec Tzannes has been recognised latterly as an exemplar of new infill design in terrace house precincts. The traditional Victorian house was successfully reinterpreted in plan and in arrangement of public elevations to work with contemporary modes of living. The development sketches and drawings have been deposited at the Mitchell Library in the State Library of New South Wales.

**LEFT:** The architect of this terrace solved the perennial problem of a dark interior by the moving the staircase from the usual location along a party wall closer to the centre of the house and crowning its upper level with a skylight. Using this device in conjunction with an open, steel-framed staircase, light can flood in where the house was previously darkest.

**ABOVE:** The committed modernist pares back structure and materials to a pure minimum, thus reinterpreting the terrace house typology for our time. At the rear of this house, architect Ian Moore has allowed the back wall to open fully to the courtyard.

**TOP RIGHT:** The contemporary bathroom addition to this Boom-style terrace has employed a long continuous skylight to allow a flood of light into the room.

**RIGHT:** In the corridor adjacent to the bathroom above, architect Virginia Kerridge has ingeniously created a void to connect the old with the new.

**OPPOSITE PAGE TOP:** This completely minimalist interpretation of the traditional composition by Ian Moore is a fine example of how modernity can co-exist with tradition.

**OPPOSITE PAGE BOTTOM:** At the rear of the terrace above, the enclosure was pared down for living space. The glazed wall, using a sliding mechanism, folds away completely to admit natural light. The generosity of the double-height space can never be matched in traditional terrace houses.

## FUNCTIONAL SOLUTIONS

Whatever its grace and charm, the design and planning of the traditional terrace house left many aspects of domestic comfort and convenience either poorly achieved or altogether unresolved. Conceived before the days of the motor car, it offered no accommodation for off-street parking. Other shortcomings include a lack of privacy between adjoining houses, poor levels of natural light penetration and ventilation, a disconnected relationship between kitchen and living areas, as well as between bathroom and bedrooms areas (often on different levels), and a clumsy connection between the interior of the house and a useful, well-designed outdoor living space. Of these problems the provision of a garage opening onto the rear lane was the simplest to solve. Bringing light into a house built on a traditional terrace allotment of between four and six metres wide and fifteen to twenty metres deep presents difficulties. Innovative solutions here lay in recasting the traditional plan and bringing the functions of the kitchen wing into the main body of the house.

By relocating the stair towards the centre of the house, rather than along a party wall, and capping it with a generous skylight, it was possible to allow in a flood of diffused light. In the past the kitchen had been relegated to a service wing at the back of the house, often beyond the back door, which swallowed up much of the potential garden area. But with modern appliances, good lighting and ducted ventilation the kitchen, bathroom and laundry no longer need to be located along external walls with windows or chimney flues. Modern materials such as structural steel and plate glass allow the imaginative architect an opportunity to create double-height spaces and to remove internal walls where required. Perhaps the greatest successes of the well-designed contemporary terrace house are well-connected indoor and outdoor living spaces and the creation of a successful garden in a very limited area.

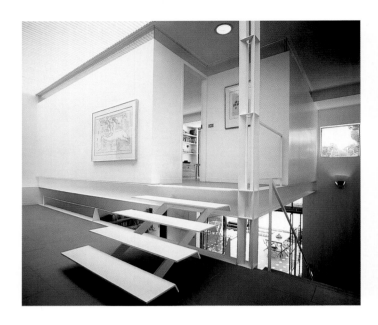

**ABOVE LEFT:** Glenn Murcutt's alterations to a Victorian terrace in Paddington, Sydney, initially attracted opposition, but the result has been recognised as a work of great architectural merit. Murcutt's solution to getting light into the interior is delightfully simple, yet successful: by lifting the split floor levels and glazing the upper sections of the internal walls he drew light into the house in a manner unimaginable in a traditional terrace house.

**ABOVE RIGHT:** In the kitchen, which is essentially underground, the workbench was pushed up against a blind wall, leaving the dining area open to the garden courtyard, allowing a more spacious feeling to an area which traditionally did not serve as an entertaining area.

**BELOW:** Murcutt kept the front façade and the remainder of the dwelling was radically rebuilt to create what is essentially a new house. The material and design of the rear of the terrace speaks confidently about the era in which it was constructed.

**RIGHT:** The relationship between the internal living space and the garden in the Magney house is a *tour de force*. Murcutt showed deft control of materials, colour and texture, light, shade, stone and water, all of which contribute a successful adaptation of this old terrace. By relating the house and garden to an attractive broader suburban setting, this modern Sydney garden is visually extended, placing the dwelling in the context of its surroundings.

## TODAY'S TERRACE GARDEN STYLES

The gardens of many contemporary terraces are deliberately minimalist, allowing the architecture of the house to dominate. Others are extremely simple but make effective use of limited space. The 'Magney' house in Paddington has a front garden in keeping with the streetscape. The simple but elegant back garden, essentially an outdoor living space, uses the concept of 'borrowed scenery' by exploiting views from the garden to the distant greenery of the opposite ridge. Espaliered lemon trees grow against a side wall, translating an established tradition of gardens into a contemporary idiom. Water is introduced in the form of a long trough. This model, where the front garden is low-key and sympathetic to the historic significance of the area while the back garden is a contemporary style with a sense of privacy and garden atmosphere, is commendable in its balance of heritage with modern taste.

Deeply set openings in thick stuccoed masonry walls and careful attention to detail are hallmarks of the contemporary terrace house. Modern lifestyles are well suited to living and entertaining spaces which flow seamlessly inside and out. The modern terrace garden needs ample hard-paved areas for sitting and dining al fresco but little in the way of planting. Here, Alec Tzannes has made a generous courtyard seem even more extensive by the use of very large sandstone flagstones.

# ACKNOWLEDGEMENTS

Many people and organisations have assisted in the preparation of this book. The authors and publisher are grateful for the help and information provided by the following:

Hector Abrahams, Bill and Mim Aldritt, Timothy Chen, Tom Chin, Terence Clarke, Alan Croker, Stephen Davies, Geoffrey Henwood, Historic Houses Trust (NSW), Ross Honeysett, Michael Jones, Peter Kennedy-Smith, Virginia Kerridge, Alan Landis, André Le Nôtre, Elisha Long, Richard Lyle, Warwick and Rosemary Mayne-Wilson of Mayne-Wilson & Associates, Ian Moore, Glenn Murcutt, Mara Barnes and the National Trust of Australia (NSW), National Trust of Australia (VIC), Jennifer Nursey, Chris Pratten, Graeme Prisk, Tony Strachan, Andrew Stuart-Robertson, Peter Todd, Alec Tzannes, Robin White, Malcolm Wilson.

In addition, the authors and publisher would like to thank:

Ellen Dickins for access to Jobbins Terrace, a conservation project of the Sydney Cove Authority; the staff at Susannah Place, Sydney, a property of the Historic Houses Trust of New South Wales; the staff at Tasma Terrace, Melbourne, a property of the National Trust of Victoria; and Susan Duyker and Geoff Bailey of the Sydney Cove Authority.

# PICTURE CREDITS

All principal photography is copyright © 1999 Lansdowne Publishing Pty Ltd, excluding the following images:

© Tom Chin: p.112; p.116 (top right and bottom).

© Ross Honeysett: p.95 (top left and bottom); p.116 (top left); p.117 (top and bottom); p.122.

© Roel Loopers/PhotoIndex: p.11 (bottom); p.65 (top); p.68 (bottom)

© Bart Maiorana: pp.110/1; p.114 (top and bottom); pp.120/1.

© Colleen Morris: p.61 (top left); p.98; p.99 (top left); p.106; p.107 (bottom right).

© Eric Sierins/Max Dupain and Associates Pty Ltd: p.118 (top left, top right and bottom); p.119.

© Alexander Tzannes Associates Pty Ltd: p.113; p.115 (top and bottom).

Archival images were obtained from:

The Archives Authority of New South Wales: p41 (top); p.44; p.47 (bottom right); p.49 (top).

Government Printing Office Collection, State Library of New South Wales: p.6.

Historic Photograph Collection, Macleay Museum, The University of Sydney: p.13 (top right).

Mitchell Library, State Library of New South Wales: p.32; p.35 (top).

Colleen Morris' book collection: p.24, p.36—from *The Floricultural Cabinet and Florist's Magazine*; p.57 (top right); p.58 (top right); p.60—from New and Beautiful-Leaved Plants; p.13 top left and bottom left illustration)—from Suburban Gardener and Villa Companion; p.25 (bottom illustration of)—from Vernacular Garden.

National Library of Australia: p.29 (top); p.31; p.33 (top right), p.37.

Private collection: p.12.

LEFT: Many local councils, designers and house owners have difficulty in determining an appropriate philosophy in the alteration and adaptation of the rear sections of terraces. The desire to renew with the need to conserve mean that radical changes require a high degree of architectural skill. At the back of this Sydney Boom-style terrace, Ian Moore has divided a terrace into two apartments. In order to connect the top apartment to the garden he built a striking three-story spiral staircase.

# GLOSSARY

**Aesthetic Movement:** A late nineteenth-century English artistic movement in painting and decorative arts that focused on purely decorative aspects, producing a fashion for 'artistic' furniture, pottery etc.

**Anthemion:** In classical architecture a stylised decorative motif derived from the flower of the honeysuckle.

**Arcading:** The linear arrangement of arches, whether segmental, half-round, or elliptical, which could be structural and freestanding, as in a loggia or verandah, or simply decorative, as on a masonry wall.

**Arts and Crafts movement:** A movement which emerged in England from the middle of the nineteenth century of writers, designers, architects and craftsmen and women who, turning their backs on industrialisation, advocated hand-wrought craft-made buildings and decorative arts and espoused a philosophy of using all materials to express their inherent qualities.

**Art Nouveau:** A movement in the arts and architecture around the turn of the twentieth century with its focus in France and Belgium, which threw off the eclectic historicism of past styles and advocated the use of flowing sinuous lines. Its followers were highly influenced by the ideas of the Arts and Crafts movement's use of materials.

**Ashlar:** Masonry of stone blocks cut to regular, typically rectangular, shapes and laid in horizontal courses.

**Balustrade:** A railing supported by balusters along the edge of a stair, verandah or balcony.

**Baluster:** A vertical member of a balustrade connecting the floor or stair tread to the handrail.

**Barge boards:** Decorated boards, often fretted, applied to the open gable end of a roof at the overhang of the eaves.

**Breakfront:** A term derived from the furniture of English cabinet-maker Thomas Chippendale (1718–79), who made bookcases with an innovative central section that 'broke' forward.

**Belvedere tower:** A lookout tower often found in larger Italianate Boom-style and Federation houses; from the Italian 'to see well'.

**Classical orders:** In classical Greek architecture the three decorative styles of the column and entablature structural system—Doric, Ionic and Corinthian—the Romans added the Tuscan and Composite orders.

**Console brackets:** Swirling brackets derived from the entablature of Ionic

and Corinthian orders of architecture.

**Cornice:** Originally one of the three principal elements of the entablature of the classical orders of architecture; also the name given to decorative plasterwork used to cover the meeting of wall and ceiling.

**Dado:** From classical architecture, either the lower section of a wall finished in wallpaper or paintwork, or a moulded timber or plaster rail which defines this part of the wall.

**Double-hung sash window:** Timber sash windows that slide vertically and are counterbalanced by weighted sash cords; Dutch in origin and first used in England by architect Sir Christopher Wren (1632–1723) at Hampton Court Palace.

**Encaustic tiles:** Industrially made coloured tiles. Part of the Gothic revival, they were based on medieval examples where different coloured clays were inlaid to form geometric patterns; derived from the Latin word to 'burn in'.

**Entablature:** In classical Greek architecture the decorative elements of the beam section of the Greek temple consisting of the architrave, frieze and cornice.

**Escutcheon:** Originally a heraldic shield but later any decorative panel holding an inscription.

**Fanlight:** A window, originally fan-shaped in Georgian architecture, located over a door, often the front door, to admit light into the hallway.

**Finial:** Originally a device in nineteenth-century Gothic architecture to decorate the top of a gable or other vertical element.

**French door:** A pair of doors, usually glazed, opening from a room to a verandah or balcony.

**French window:** An oversized double-hung timber-framed window with vertically sliding sashes where the sill is at floor level opening to a verandah or balcony.

**Frieze:** Originally part of the entablature in the classical orders of architecture, any element inside or out sitting immediately below the cornice.

**Gable:** A type of timber-framed roof where the edge of the roof ends in a triangular form.

**Golden Section:** A ratio of approx. 1:1.6 based on classical proportions which, it was thought, produced rectangles of perfect harmony.

**Gothic:** A style of medieval ecclesiastical architecture, originally in France, used throughout Europe from c. 1200 to 1500 and

characterised by the use of the pointed arch and ribbed vault.

**Gothic revival:** An architectural movement in England in the mid-eighteenth century which advocated rejection of the classical style in favour of a revival of the medieval style.

**Hipped (roof):** A form of construction where the roof slopes down at the same pitch on all sides of the building, avoiding the use of open gables at the ends.

**Infill:** A building constructed on an empty site between two existing structures.

**Joist:** A structural timber to which floorboards or ceiling are attached for support.

**Margin bar:** A form of glazing bar which for aesthetic reasons was located off-centre; common in Regency-style French doors.

**Marseilles tile:** An interlocking patterned terracotta roofing tile which was popular in Federation architecture, originally imported from Marseilles, France.

**Modelling:** The manner in which the shape of a building, its elements and spaces, are defined.

**Modillion:** Derived from classical architecture, a series of decorative blocks or brackets forming part of a cornice.

**Moulding:** A shaped decorative profile, originally derived from classical architecture.

**Ornamentation:** Any decorative element added to a building.

**Parapet:** The vertical extension of an exterior wall continued to hide the line of the roof.

**Party wall:** A common wall, usually on the side boundary, shared by adjoining houses.

**Paterae:** Circular stylised flowers derived from classical architecture used as ornamentation on a building.

**Picturesque style:** Originating in eighteenth-century landscape design, an architectural style in which irregularity of form, profile and massing replace classical ideas of balance, symmetry and rhythm.

**Polychrome (brickwork):** Of more than one colour; when applied to masonry it refers to a stylistic trend of the Gothic revival movement.

**Quoins:** Alternating large and small blocks of ashlar or stucco applied for emphasis to the corners of a building or at door and window openings.

**Repoussé:** Decorative metalwork, usually copperware, hammered from the back; from the French meaning 'raised in relief'.

**Rubble work:** A rough form of masonry, in contrast to ashlar, with stones of a random shape or roughly squared, usually laid irregularly without courses.

**Rustication:** A decorative treatment of ashlar, or stucco imitating ashlar, with a roughened surface, often with deep-cut joints to throw shadow lines.

**Sandstock:** Soft bricks, often of a pinkish salmon colour, made by pressing a clay mixture into timber moulds lined with sand to prevent sticking.

**Segmental pediment:** Of classical origin, but later a favoured device of Baroque architecture, a pediment formed by a segment of a circle.

**Shingle:** A piece of split timber used instead of tiles to clad roofs of Australian buildings until early 1870s, usually a casuarina when used near the coast.

**String course:** A horizontal moulding in external brick or stonework, often level with an internal upper floor or a window sill.

**Stucco:** A lime or cement-based plaster or render applied to the exterior of a building, traditionally in imitation of ashlar stonework.

**Swag:** An ornamental device derived from classical architecture consisting of a drooping garland of fruits, flowers and foliage.

**Terracotta:** Fired ceramic material of reddish-orange, often unglazed, used in making Marseilles pattern roof tiles and other architectural features such as chimney pots and urns.

**Valance:** A decorative panel or strip of timber or cast iron applied below the eaves of a verandah roof.

**Vermiculation:** A carved decorative pattern applied to masonry, or imitated in stucco, which resembles the holes that worms might eat; from the Latin for 'worm eaten'.

**Tuscan order:** A Roman order of architecture derived from the Etruscans who had simplified the Greek Doric order by removing the fluting, altering the capital and adding a base.

**Window sash:** A timber frame holding the glass of a window pane, rather than the frame into which the sash sits.

# SELECT BIBLIOGRAPHY

APPERLY, Richard, IRVING, Roberts and REYNOLDS, Peter, *A Pictorial Guide to Identifying Australian Architecture*, Angus & Robertson, Sydney, 1989.

BATEY, Mavis, *Regency Gardens*, Shire Publications, Buckinghamshire, UK, 1995.

BOYD, Robin, *Australia's Home: Why Australians Built Their Homes The Way They Did*, Melbourne University Press, 1952.

BUNCE, Daniel, 1836 *Catalogue, of Seeds and Plants, indigenous and exotic, cultivated and on sale at Denmark Hill Nursery, Newtown Road, Hobart town*, Mulini Press, Canberra, 1994.

BURTON, Craig Anthony, 'Housing the Glebe—Architects, Builders and Styles 1828–1915' unpublished M.A. thesis University of Sydney, 1979.

COX, Philip, & LUCAS, Clive, *Australian Colonial Architecture*, Lansdowne Publishing, Sydney, 1978.

CUFFLEY, Peter, *Cottage Gardens in Australia*, The Five Mile Press, Canterbury Victoria, 1983.

CUFFLEY, Peter, *Traditional Gardens in Australia, Creating Your Own Period Garden*, The Five Mile Press, Victoria, 1991.

EVANS, IAN, *The Federation House: a Restoration Guide*, Flannel Flower Press, Sydney, 1986.

——, *Getting the Details Right: Restoring Australian Houses 1890s–1920s*, Flannel Flower Press, Department of Planning of New South Wales, 1989.

FOWLES, Joseph, *Sydney in 1848*, facsimile edn., Ure Smith in conjunction with National Trust of Australia (NSW), 1973.

FRASER, Hugh, *The Federation House*, Australia's Own Style, Lansdowne Publishing, Sydney, 1986.

FREELAND, J.M., *Architecture in Australia: a History*, Penguin Books, Victoria, 1972.

GIROUARD, Marks, *Sweetness & Light: The 'Queen Anne' Movement, 1860–1900*, Clarendon Press, Oxford, 1977.

HASTINGS RIVER HISTORICAL SOCIETY, *Annabella Boswell's Journal, Life in the 1830s and 1840s*, Angus & Robertson, Sydney, 1965.

HIBBERD, Shirley, *New and Rare Beautiful-Leaved Plants*, Bell and Daldy, London, 1870.

HORTICULTURAL SOCIETY OF SYDNEY, *Horticultural Magazine and Gardener's Calendar of New South Wales*, John Gelding, George Street Markets, Sydney, 1864, 1865, 1866, 1867.

HOWELLS, Trevor, and NICHOLSON, Michael, *Towards the Dawn: Federation Architecture in Australia, 1890–1915*, Hale & Ironmonger, Sydney, 1993.

HUNT, John Dixon and WOLSCHKE-BULMAHN, Joachim (eds.), *The Vernacular Garden, Dumbarton Oaks Colloquium on the History of Landscape Architecture*, XIV, Dumbarton Oaks Research Library and Collection, Washington, D.C., 1993.

IRVING, Robert, comp., *The History and Design of the Australian House*, Oxford University Press, Melbourne, 1985.

JONES, James, 'Diary of the Head Gardener 1884–89', Royal Botanic Gardens, unpublished manuscript AO2/8558.

KARSKENS, Grace, *The Rocks: Life in Early Sydney*, Melbourne University Press, 1997.

KELLY, Max, *Faces in the Street: William Street Sydney 1916*, Doak Press, Sydney, 1978.

——, *Paddock Full of Houses: Paddington, 1840–1890*, Doak Press, Sydney, 1978.

KEMP, Edward, *How To Lay Out a Garden*, 3rd Edition, Bradbury, Evans & Co., London, 1865.

KERR, James Semple, *The Conservation Plan*, National Trust of Australia (New South Wales), Sydney, 1996.

LOUDON, John Claudius, *The Suburban Gardener and Villa Companion*, Orme, Brown, Green and Longmans, London and W. Black, Edinburgh, 1838.

LOUDON, John Claudius, *The Gardener's Magazine*, Vol. VI, January 1840.

McPHEE, John, *Australian Decorative Arts in the Australian National Gallery*, Australian National Gallery, Canberra, 1982.

MOLYNEUX, Ian, *Looking Around Perth*, Westcolour Press in association with the Western Australian Chapter of the Royal Australian Institute of Architects, East Fremantle, 1981.

MOORE, Robert, BURKE, Sheridan & JOYCE, Ray, *Australian Cottages*, Lansdowne Publishing, Sydney, 1993.

MULTHUSIUS, Stefan, *The English Terrace House*, Yale University Press, New Haven and London, 1982.

NOTTLE, Trevor, *The Cottage Garden Revived*, Kangaroo Press, Sydney, 1984.

NOTTLE, Trevor and JARRATT, Ray, *Old-Fashioned Gardens*, Kangaroo Press, Sydney, 1992.

PETERSON, Richard, for the National Trust of Australia (Victoria), *Fences & Gates c.1840–1925*, Technical Bulletin 8.1, National Trust of Australia (Victoria), 1988

RUSKIN, John, *The Seven Lamps of Architecture*, Elder Smith, London, 1849.

SMITH, Bernard & Kate, *The Architectural Character of Glebe*, Sydney University Press, Sydney, 1973.

STAPLETON, Ian, EVANS, Ian & LUCAS, Clive, *Colour Schemes for Old Australian Houses*, Flannel Flower Press, Sydney, 1984.

——, *More Colour Schemes for Old Australian Houses*, Flannel Flower Press, Sydney, 1984.

TURNER, Brian, *The Australian Terrace House*, Angus & Robertson, Sydney, 1995.

WALKER, Meredith and MARQUIS, Kyle, *The Illustrated Burra Charter*, National Trust of Australia (New South Wales), 1996.

WATTS, Peter, *Historic Gardens of Victoria, a Reconnaissance*, Oxford University Press, Melbourne, 1983.

WILSON, William Hardy, *Old Colonial Architecture in New South Wales and Tasmania*, W. Hardy Wilson, Sydney, 1924.

# INDEX

# INDEX

The *Magnolia* is a genus containing
a number of species which are
suited for cultivation in the small
gardens of terrace houses. They are
beautiful small trees or shrubs with
delicate blooms in various shades.